ENGLAND

THE OFFICIAL HISTORY

Published in 2021 by Welbeck

An Imprint of Welbeck Non-Fiction Limited, part of Welbeck Publishing Group.

Based in London and Sydney.

www.welbeckpublishing.com

Text © Welbeck Non-Fiction Limited, part of Welbeck Publishing Group.

Published under license for © The Football Association Ltd

A CIP catalogue record for this book is available from the British Library

ISBN 978 1 78739 902 0

Editor: Ross Hamilton
Design: Russell Knowles & James Pople
Picture Research: Paul Langan
Production: Arlene Alexander

Printed in Great Britain

10 9 8 7 6 5 4 3 2 1

Every effort has been made to ensure that this publication is as factually correct as possible, and all statistics have been confirmed and verified to the best of our ability. We're grateful for any feedback regarding the content contained herein, as we strive to maintain the highest editorial standards. Welbeck Publishing apologises for any unintentional errors or omissions, which will be corrected in future editions of this book.

Front cover photographs: (Bobby Moore) Bentley Archive/Popperfoto/Getty Images; (Wembley Stadium) Matt McNulty/Manchester City/Getty Images; (David Beckham) Mike Hewitt/Getty Images; (Kelly Smith) Lars Baron/FIFA/Getty Images; (John Barnes) Mark Leech/Offside/Getty Images; (Harry Kane) Alex Morton/UEFA/Getty Images; (Steph Houghton) Robert Cianflone/Getty Images; (Peter Shilton) David Cannon/Getty Images; (Alex Scott) Martin Rose/Getty Images; (Wayne Rooney) Getty Images/The FA.
Back cover photographs: (Alf Ramsey) Hulton Archive/Getty Images; (England huddle) Lynne Cameron/The FA; (Viv Anderson) Simon Bruty/Getty Images; (England fans at Euro96) Allsport/Getty Images; (England celebration versus Denmark) Eddie Keogh/Getty Images/The FA; (Fara Williams) Getty Images/The FA; (Bobby Charlton) Rolls Press/Popperfoto/Getty Images; (Wembley Stadium) Peter King/Fox Photos/Getty Images; (Paul Gascoigne) Stu Forster/Getty Images.

ENGLAND

THE OFFICIAL HISTORY

DANIEL STOREY

FOREWORDS BY

TONY ADAMS & FARA WILLIAMS

WELBECK

CONTENTS

Following pages: England celebrate their Euro 2020 semi-final victory over Denmark at Wembley Stadium, which saw the men's team reach their first major final in 55 years.

FOREWORD

TONY ADAMS

Captaining England remains the ultimate footballing achievement for any sportsman or woman. When I reflect upon the privilege of leading out the national team at Wembley during Euro '96, with the hopes of the country on our shoulders and the mood surrounding the England team changing as we progressed through the tournament, it makes me incredibly emotional. When you wear that armband, you become immediately aware of just how much this means to so many. That pressure can only inspire every England player on the pitch: the fans become our engine, our motor to perform. Our country belongs to all of us and we genuinely feel together – players, fans: England.

I know the hard times of playing for England; I am happy to talk about them now because I hope my experience can help others. The European Championship in 1988 was my first major international tournament, I was 21 years old, and I had a torrid time against Marco van Basten and the Dutch. I was not selected for Italia '90, was injured in 1992 and then we failed to qualify for the World Cup in 1994. Preparing for

Euro '96, after eight long years, gave me the focus I needed, something to aim towards. I will never forget beating the Netherlands at Wembley that glorious summer. It was a personal redemption for me after 1988.

I hope that today's stars are able to look after themselves. The pressure and the scrutiny of playing for England has only grown with the advent of social media and rolling news coverage. Fortunately, there is far more help for players who come under that spotlight, and the Football Association and England setup deserve great credit for that.

Having been there, I know that those players talented and lucky enough to wear the England shirt understand the position of privilege they are in. Rest assured, even with all the money in the club game and the pressures of living in the public eye, this is the pinnacle. And however all-encompassing the mania of club football threatens to be, nothing will ever match the pride you feel representing your country, with millions of people depending upon 11 players and a manager to shape the national mood.

FOREWORD
FARA WILLIAMS

Playing football for England was all I ever wanted, and something I never dreamed might be possible. I was lucky enough to enjoy a 20-year career with success at club and international level, but the moment I always return to was making my home debut for England in a 3–0 win over Portugal in Portsmouth. That's when it really hammered home what it meant to play for your country.

My journey in football hasn't always been easy. Like many female players in England, my early years – before the game was fully professional – were incredibly difficult. There just wasn't the support network for young hopefuls that exists now, but I firmly believe that helped make me the player I was and the person I am; those struggles are what give us the steel to keep striving for success and the motivation to make the most of our time at the top.

Playing for England over a period of 15 years allowed me to bear witness to the rise of the women's game in this country. In 2002, we played Iceland in front of 3,000 people in Birmingham, but by 2014 there were 45,000 people in Wembley watching us face Germany. As players, we were all incredibly proud to play a small part in that process, inspiring young girls to dream that professional football is a possibility. We understood that we were not just achieving in the moment but aiming to create a legacy for those who stand on our shoulders and walk in our footsteps.

And the structure around the team did change. When I made my first appearance, England had only qualified for one of the three Women's World Cups and were struggling to qualify for the 2003 tournament. From that point on, I was fortunate enough to go to three World Cups in a row and captain my country in Canada in 2015. After my debut, the best moment for me was leading the England team to the World Cup semi-finals for the first time in 2015. The semi-final defeat against Japan was hard to take, but scoring the winning penalty in the third-place play-off against Germany was a true mark of our progress. Before then we had faced Germany eight times since I made my debut, and never won.

There will always be more to do. The pursuit of equality will never stop. Women's football in this country was forced to begin its modern form from several steps behind the start line and thus we will forever have to work harder and longer for our progress. But we are making that progress. Those who pull on that famous Lionesses shirt can never lose sight of their role in helping that journey. And you never forget how it made you feel.

INTRODUCTION

On Sunday July 11, 2021, 54,280 days since England's first official international, the men's national team played its 1,021st official match – and its second major tournament final. If England was indeed the birthplace of modern football, there have been many decades when we yearned for it to come home and waited fruitlessly for the sound of footsteps on the front mat and a knock on the door.

For all the dominance of the club game on the football calendar, nothing captures the interest of the nation quite like, and for quite as long as, international football. The most watched event in the history of British broadcasting was not a royal wedding, the opening ceremony of the Olympics, or the climax to a soap opera story, but a football match: 32.3 million people watched England win the 1966 World Cup Final. In 1998, 2004, 2006, 2014, 2018 and 2021, the most viewed television events of the year were all international games.

Club football may demand great loyalty and increasingly extreme emotional reactions, but major tournaments drive the country into a patriotic frenzy. We throng together in pubs and bars and in town squares and parks to watch and wait and hope to celebrate. We greet our fellow compatriots as if they were friends reunited from our childhood simply because they're as excited as us. We convince ourselves of nonsensical superstitions that are both objectively meaningless and yet mean the world. Front pages and back pages are dedicated to the same stories. The main bulletins of the evening news reports pass on information about strained muscles, fractured bones and predict the mindset of the manager, who becomes the temporary de facto leader of the land.

England have had their share of heartache and disappointment: Diego Maradona's hand and then left foot; the defeat to the USA in 1950 that was assumed to be a mistake, so shocking was the result; Ellen White's disallowed goal against the same nation in 2019; Croatia in 2007, Iceland in 2016 and Germany more times than anyone would care to mention. And the penalties – all those penalties: 1984, 1990, 1996, 1998, 2004, 2006, 2012, 2021. Each time we believed it might be different.

The England men's and women's teams have played in 20 World Cups and 18 European Championships and they have won only one. Those tournaments have been pockmarked by setbacks, injuries and red cards, as well as missed chances, mistakes and a thousand other things that on other days might just have gone our way.

But then this was never only about victory. We follow football, and we follow England, not just because we think that we should win or will win or we might ever win again, but because we're desperate to be a part of something that may end up with us winning – and we wouldn't miss it for the world in case we do. The triumphant moments, those days when we can bask in the glow of a team fulfilling its potential, are elevated by their sheer rarity.

Opposite: Geoff Hurst scores England's third goal against West Germany in the 1966 World Cup Final at Wembley Stadium, arguably the most famous strike in the history of the team.

Right, from top: Stanley Matthews, one of England's first superstars, plays against Scotland at Wembley in March 1944; Alf Ramsey is presented with the Jules Rimet Trophy by his captain Bobby Moore; Hope Powell, one of the most important figures in the shaping of the modern Lionesses, takes a training session in 2002.

Above: Gareth Southgate has become emblematic of the Three Lions as both a player (above) and manager (below).

Opposite: Lionesses stars such as Ellen White (above), Jill Scott and Nikita Parris (below) have stood on the shoulders of their trailblazing predecessors to help propel the women's game to new heights.

Following pages: At the 2015 Women's World Cup, the Lionesses recorded the best England tournament performance since 1966, beating Germany in the third-place play-off.

England's history begins with a trip to Scotland in November 1872, a collection of amateur players who travelled through the night after honorary Football Association secretary Charles Alcock had placed an advert in several Scottish newspapers to try and arrange a fixture. Alcock was the first great visionary of English football, but he could have had no sense of the global phenomenon he had seeded.

In its infancy, the England men's team played in an age of repetition. Matches against the same small group of home-nation opponents marked the beginning of a deliberate isolationism that eventually forced them to begin their quest for major tournament success from behind the start line. But glory then came quickly: just 16 years after their first World Cup match, England lifted the trophy on the greatest day in our country's sporting history.

It did not lead to the age of dominance that many hoped for and too many assumed would occur. England perennially struggled in the sapping heat of summer tournaments played far from home. Debates about the standard of coaching, level of training, prioritisation of physicality and the maximum wage warped over time into arguments over the influx of foreign players, the rising dominance of the club game and the shortage of high-class managers to take England one step closer to the salvation they craved. As the years ticked by, the hurt only grew and the discourse became more fierce.

In the women's game, an altogether more obvious barrier was finally removed. The success of women's football at the start of the 20th century had been viewed as a threat to the men's game and so was banned for a period of 50 years. Exactly 100 years after England's first international against Scotland, the women's side faced the same opponents.

The rise in the popularity of women's football since then has been extraordinary. Those pioneers of the women's game in this country – Tommy Tranter, Martin Reagan, Hope Powell, Gillian Coultard and Sheila Parker – deserve their namecheck here. In the men's game, players and coaches were simply striving for the top; the greats of the England women's team first had to build the ladder from which they could hope to one day even see it. Now they aim, as with the men's team, to sit on top of the world and breathe the heightened air that only major tournament success can bring.

This book aims to chart the history of those two teams, glorious and otherwise. It tells the story of the men's side, from their first match in Partick to the final of Euro 2020 at Wembley Stadium in 2021, and the women's team's rise to prominence following their belated beginning.

It's an account of brilliant coaches, generous managers and astonishing trailblazers who allowed others to stand on their shoulders, as well as majestically talented players, many of whom achieved greatness in the club game but all of whom retired knowing that pulling on an England shirt was the pinnacle. It is a tribute to those who fought for equality, fought for their country and fought for their right to be heard and taken seriously. It is a tale of occasional triumph, regular despair and eternal hope. It is the story of two teams, united by one shirt and three lions.

Daniel Storey, 2021

CHAPTER ONE

THE DAWN OF A TEAM

1870s – 1890s

FOOTBALL IS JUST A GAME – BUT ALSO FAR MORE THAN A GAME. IT HAS BECOME A UNIVERSAL FORCE, A CULTURAL RELIGION THAT EXTENDS TO THE FURTHEST CORNERS OF THE GLOBE AND PROVOKES SIMILAR EMOTIVE RESPONSES IN EACH ONE. THE FÉDÉRATION INTERNATIONALE DE FOOTBALL ASSOCIATION (FIFA) HAS 18 MORE MEMBER NATIONS THAN THE UNITED NATIONS. AN AUDIENCE OF 3.572 BILLION WATCHED AT LEAST PART OF THE 2018 WORLD CUP IN RUSSIA, ALMOST HALF THE PEOPLE ON EARTH; NOTHING COMMANDS AS GREAT AN AUDIENCE AS INTERNATIONAL FOOTBALL. NOVEMBER 30, 1872, WAS ITS BIRTHDATE.

It had been raining for three days, but Saturday morning in Scotland brought relieving news. The downpour had become a drizzle that turned into milky early winter sunshine, albeit accompanied by a thick mist that would briefly delay the start of what would become football's oldest rivalry. When you stand on the verge of creating history, what does 20 more minutes matter?

As midday ticked over into early afternoon, supporters began to gather at Hamilton Crescent, a ground to the north west of Glasgow that the West of Scotland cricket club still calls home. Official records differ, with attendance estimates ranging from 2,500 to 4,000. All gentlemen paid a shilling; ladies – of which there were many – watched for free.

It had not been an easy event to arrange. An 800-mile round trip by rail, often travelling through the night on hard seats in loud and draughty carriages, was far from ideal preparation for a sporting contest. Then there was the prohibitive cost of the exercise. England made it work because, perhaps even subconsciously, they foresaw the importance of the occasion.

As it turned out, the first official international match was goalless, although not without incident or intrigue. Scotland, their team selected by, and largely from, its most successful club, Queen's Park, operated with a passing style that pegged England back in the first half. Robert Leckie had a shot tipped over the tape (goal nets and crossbars were yet to be introduced) and the crowd mistakenly roared for a goal.

But as the game wore on, England's preference for power (the *Glasgow Herald* reported that England were two stone heavier per man, on average) allowed them to dominate on a pitch that was becoming tacky after the wet weather. Charles Chenery and Arnold Kirke Smith both hit the post and Cuthbert Ottaway – still England's fourth-

Above: Charles Alcock (1842–1907), FA Secretary between 1870 and 1895 and a key instigator of the formation of the England national team.

Opposite: Promotional poster for the first international match, played between England and Scotland in November 1872.

INTERNATIONAL FOOT-BALL MATCH,

(ASSOCIATION RULES,)

ENGLAND *v.* SCOTLAND,

WEST OF SCOTLAND CRICKET GROUND,

HAMILTON CRESCENT, PARTICK,

SATURDAY, 30th November, 1872, at 2 p.m.

ADMISSION—ONE SHILLING.

youngest captain – dribbled past players to the wonder of onlookers who had arrived unsure of what to expect from a sport overshadowed in Scotland by the popularity of rugby.

There may have been long-established historical reasons for a grudge to form between teams from either side of the border, but the match was played in wonderful spirit. When referee William Keay signalled the end of the game, supporters enthusiastically applauded those in both white and dark blue for a fair, determined and respectful contest. Scotland's players gave three cheers to their counterparts. By the time the two sides had enjoyed dinner together in Carrick's Royal Hotel, England decided to repay the honour. It was agreed that the game would become a regular occurrence.

November 1872 may have marked England's first official international, but it was neither their first fixture nor the first time they had faced Scotland. In 1870, Wanderers footballer and honorary Football Association secretary Charles Alcock placed an advert in several Scottish newspapers suggesting an international fixture between the two countries. But with Scottish clubs unconvinced and unwilling to send a team to London, Alcock and England were forced to make do with a team of Scottish players based at English clubs. Five matches were played between March 1870 and February 1872 – all were deemed unofficial.

Alcock's trailblazing role cannot be overstated. Initially working as a shipping merchant, he immersed himself in sports administration and became a visionary for the potential popularity and cultural sway of football. It was Alcock who lobbied Scotland for an official match and he who captained England in all five unofficial games. Having missed the November 1872 fixture through injury, Alcock was finally present in 1875, captaining and scoring for England in a 2–2 draw that would be his only recognised international cap.

Alcock's most famous creation was the FA Cup in 1871, a new national competition that forged relationships and rivalries between pockets of clubs in different parts of the country. In the first edition of the Cup, Queen's Park reached the semi-finals and travelled to London to face Wanderers at the Kennington Oval. That journey helped persuade Scottish clubs of the benefits of an international fixture.

Over the course of its first two decades in international football, the England team led a relatively nomadic existence. There was no designated national stadium; they played Scotland at the Kennington Oval in London, Bramall Lane in Sheffield and Leamington Road in Blackburn, as well as home games at Alexandra Meadows, Whalley Range and Aigburth cricket ground in Blackburn, Manchester and Liverpool respectively. This represented a determination to arrange fixtures in northern towns where football was gaining mass popularity among the working class.

The same characteristic was reflected in the England team itself. With the FA board picking the team – nominally led by Alcock – priority was often given to players based in the Midlands and the North to try and expand the FA Cup. In their first 22 international fixtures, England gave caps to 100 different players.

One feature of England's international infancy was Scotland's dominance. The Scots won 10 of the first 16 meetings, including crushing 7–2 and 6–1 victories in 1878 and 1881 respectively. England won just two. Opinion at the time suggested that Scotland's teamwork and passing were the key to their success, while England relied too heavily on individual dribbling and physical dominance. England's way of playing was hard to shift, indoctrinated on the pitches of English public schools that promoted individuality and a certain arrogance.

Opposite: Hand-coloured engraving portraying action from England's first international match against Scotland.

Above: Coloured drawing of a collection of England players wearing club colours. Norman Bailey, the first player to make more than ten appearances for England, is seated centrally, holding a ball.

Below: England team photo prior to a match against Scotland on April 6, 1891. England won 2–1. L–R, back row: S. Widdowson (linesman), R. Howarth, R. Holmes, A. Shelton, unnamed referee. Middle row: A. Smith, J. Goodall, F. Geary, E. Chadwick, A. Milward. Front row: W.I. Bassett, W.R. Moon and J. Holt.

sides of the debate, professionalism – being paid to play – was formally accepted. Three years later, the Football League was founded.

The other notable shift in policy came in 1887 with the formation of a selection committee to pick England squads. Replacing the FA board, seven men were asked to pick the England team and inevitably brought a breadth of opinion that allowed for a greater diversification of players and styles previously unseen in England teams.

With it came predictable improvement. With Northern-based players more likely to shun the traditional dribbling style of public-school English football, able to train more often to improve teamwork and tactical understanding, and with the added influence of Scottish imports that littered many provincial teams in the 1880s, the England team reaped the rewards. They shared victory with Scotland in the British Home Championship, an annual tournament between the four home nations that was established in 1883 and would run until 1984, in 1886 and were crowned champions for the first time in 1888.

That year, England won in Scotland for the first time, 5–0 at Cathkin Park in Glasgow. The team contained three players from Preston North End and one each from Wolverhampton Wanderers, Aston Villa, Accrington and West Bromwich Albion. All four forwards scored goals, viewed by journalists as proof of a leap in England's tactical interplay. No longer would class rule selection.

The nomadic existence of the England team's early years faded towards the turn of the century, but the huge turnover in players was still commonplace. By way of example, England's first match in 1889 contained only three players to have appeared in their last game in 1888. With the British Home Championship providing the only source of regular fixtures, England played 40 matches between 1872 and 1890, as many as might be covered by a four-year cycle today. The turnover of players is demonstrated by the fact that between 1872 and 1938, Blackburn Rovers full-back Bob Crompton was the only player to reach 30 caps.

But a few players were able to establish themselves as household names. Billy Bassett was a frail winger whose unique dribbling style earned him 16 caps that yielded eight goals and made him something of a celebrity. Gilbert Oswald Smith was a dynamic, versatile forward who became a star for Corinthians, the most famous amateur club in the game's history.

But above them all stood Steve Bloomer, still the second-highest goalscorer of all time in England's top flight, after Jimmy Greaves. Bloomer had remarkable ability and unerring accuracy with both feet and specialised in shooting into the bottom corner of the goal to take advantage of goalkeepers' inability to dive low quickly enough.

Bloomer made his international debut in a 9–0 win against Ireland in 1895 and scored in all of his first 10 appearances for England. No player has ever matched that consecutive scoring run. He also became the first player to score multiple hat-tricks, or score four and five goals in a match for England.

Having founded rivalries with their neighbours through the British Home Championship, England's next step was to take on foreign

Progress came not from enlightenment, but conflict. It was seeded in 1879 with Lancashire-based Darwen reaching the quarter-finals of the FA Cup with two Scottish players in the team. Darwen denied that Fergie Suter and Jimmy Love were being paid, but both had far better jobs than in Scotland and had benefit matches arranged for them by the club, thus helping them to bypass laws on enforced amateurism. Later, in 1883, Blackburn Olympic became the first northern-based team to win the FA Cup, while neighbours Blackburn Rovers won the following three editions. The influence of Scottish players and managers – Blackburn Rovers' first manager, Tom Mitchell, was a Scot – allowed for the Scottish 'passing' system to take root and thrive.

Darwen were merely one of a number Northern clubs whose working-class players could not afford to commit to football as more than a hobbyist pursuit, in contrast with the public school ethos of the South that cherished the Corinthian spirit of the amateur and aspired to play on purely gentlemanly terms, without payment. But if football was going to evolve from a mere pastime, the Northern clubs believed, players must be paid. By 1885, after bitterness and division on both

Left: Billy Bassett, outside right who scored eight goals in 16 England appearances and became one of the first celebrity footballers.

Opposite: An illustrated selection of portraits showing England's team for a match against Scotland in 1892.

> **"FOOTBALL WAS THRIVING, AIDED BY THE FORMATION OF AN OFFICIAL DOMESTIC LEAGUE AND CUP, AND DRIVEN BY ALCOCK'S DETERMINATION TO CREATE AN INTERNATIONAL FOOTBALL CALENDAR."**

opposition as a bid to both spread the gospel of football across the world and to learn techniques and tactics from other footballing cultures. Their first match against foreign opposition – albeit in an unofficial international – was during Canada's mammoth 58-match tour of the United Kingdom in 1891. A team made up of Canadians and Americans were beaten 6–1 at the Kennington Oval.

More notable unofficial friendlies came during a Football Association-arranged tour of Germany and Austria in 1899. England beat a Germany team 13–2 in Berlin before a much-changed German side were thumped 10–2. England then played a combined Austrian-German XI in two matches in Prague and Karlsruhe, winning 6–0 and 7–0 in front of meagre crowds. These comprehensive victories were explained by the Football Association deliberately taking a strong 14-man squad on their first-ever tour, while their opponents were mostly local players.

All the while, football's dominance over the winter sporting schedule was increasing and the construction of larger stadiums for league clubs led to a dramatic rise in attendances. The 12-team Football League had crowds totalling 600,000 during its inaugural season but had reached five million in 1905–06. Before 1885, no FA Cup Final attendance had surpassed 10,000 but the last final of the 19th century was watched by 73,833 spectators at Crystal Palace.

That boom was reflected in international interest. England's British Home Championship match against Scotland at Ewood Park in April 1891 drew 31,000 supporters, rising to 42,500 when England faced the same opponents at Everton's Goodison Park in April 1895. By April 1900, 63,000 were packed into Glasgow's Celtic Park to watch Scotland dismantle their old foe 4–1.

Football was thriving, aided by the formation of an official domestic league and cup, and driven by Alcock's determination to create an international football calendar. By the turn of the century, England and Scotland were locked on nine British Home Championships apiece and the England team was regularly being filled with representatives from clubs whose names are now synonymous with modern football: Burnley, Aston Villa, Sheffield United, Southampton, Liverpool, Nottingham Forest. An amateur public school pursuit had now become the cultural obsession of the masses.

Opposite: Steve Bloomer, who scored in his first 10 internationals for England (still a record) and ended his career with 28 goals in 23 matches for England.

Above: England team photo from their first tour of Germany and Austria in 1899. They won all four matches, scoring 36 goals.

PROFILE:
CHARLES ALCOCK

England's sporting history is littered with trailblazers and visionaries. Invention usually comes incrementally but occasionally someone takes a giant leap forward, allowing those who follow to stand on the shoulders of giants. In that group, none stand taller than Charles Alcock, the great "Creator" of English sport. By the time Alcock had passed away in comfort in Brighton in 1907 he had fathered eight children. You can add England's most famous trophies – the FA Cup and the Ashes urn – to his family tree.

Alcock was born into privilege, from which the opportunity for influence was afforded. Growing up in Sunderland as the son of a successful shipbuilder, the family moved to a mansion they named Sunny Side on the corner of Kings Head Hill and Woodberry Way in Chingford when Alcock was eight. Eventually standing 5ft 11in tall and weighing more than 13st with a kind, moustachioed face, he was every bit the stereotypical image of the English gentleman.

Alcock was educated at Harrow School, where he was given the chance to participate in a variety of sports. He was also schooled in the dribbling style of football that was favoured at public schools at the time – Harrow, Eton, Winchester – although all played with slightly different sets of rules.

But Alcock quickly appreciated that football's divided status in England, roughly split between the north and south and, more pertinently, between upper and working classes, had to be healed to promote a harmonising of styles and popularity of participation. Without it, one class would play a form of the game alien to the other and football may have remained a preserve of the elite.

With two friends, Alcock founded the Forest Club in the 1860s and invited locals from all backgrounds to play together. With the club playing fixtures in several locations across London, they became known as Wanderers. Not only did Alcock create the FA Cup, based on the inter-house knockout competitions he had enjoyed at Harrow, he also captained Wanderers to victory in the first final.

Organised football remained a winter sport among the upper class because of cricket's growing domination over the summer calendar. Here too, Alcock's influence was decisive. He played for Middlesex and Essex, organised the first Test match in England against an Australian touring side, became a long-serving secretary of Surrey and edited the *Cricket* newspaper for 25 years.

In hindsight, the breadth of Alcock's influence in football was astonishing, a testament to his love for the game and his tireless desire to shape its future. As well as playing for, scoring for and captaining England, and leading Wanderers to FA Cup success,

Opposite: Portrait of Charles Alcock, the great "Creator" of English sport.

Below left: Promotional poster for Surrey vs Australia cricket match in July 1888.

Below right: Vintage illustration of Alcock on the cover of *Man of the World*, published in London on February 8, 1890.

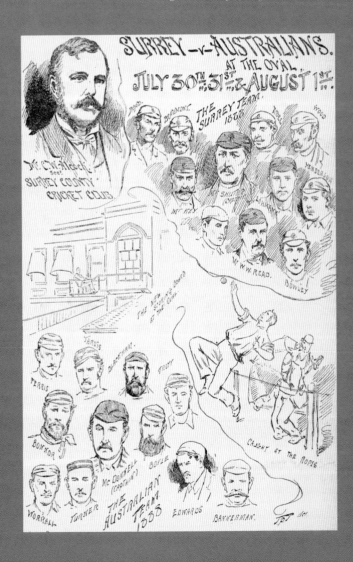

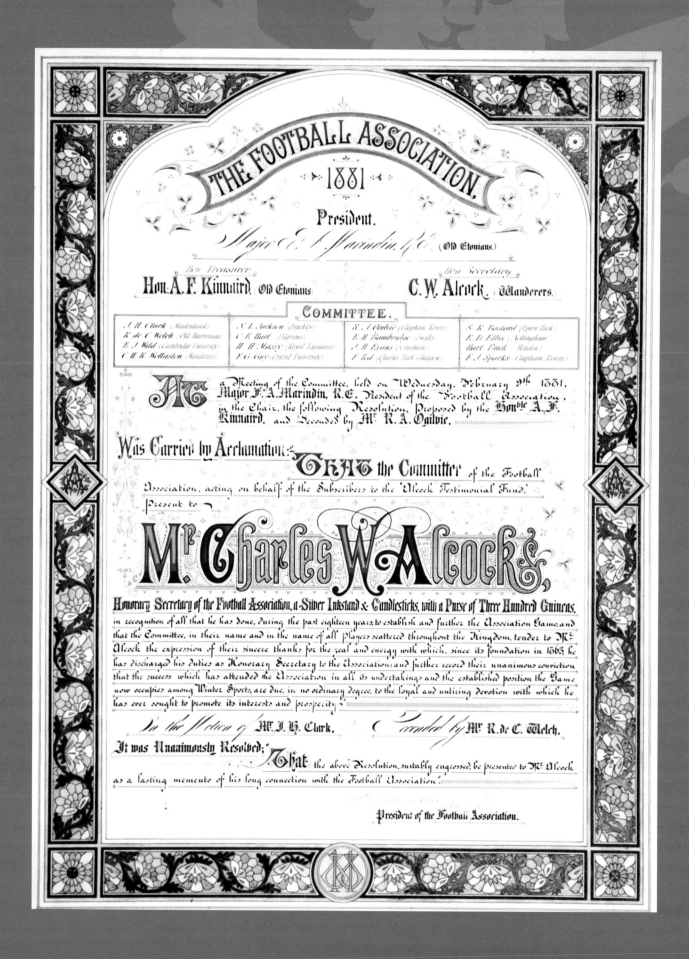

Alcock refereed the 1875 and 1879 finals. At the FA he became a master of all trades, serving as a committee member, honorary secretary, treasurer and vice president.

In part those roles and that influence was reflective of Alcock's class. But unlike many of his peers, who largely reflected the typical insularity and protectionism of the upper classes in late Victorian England, Alcock continued to understand and promote ideals of inclusivity and the potential universality of football. While not formally responsible for the introduction of professionalism, a topic on which the FA of the time were initially highly sceptical, the rise of the provincial, northern clubs who campaigned so strongly for professionalism would not have been possible without Alcock's FA Cup master stroke.

If forming the bedrock of the game's administration wasn't enough, Alcock's receptiveness to innovation was reflected on the pitch, too. Having watched Scotland repeatedly dominate England with a passing style in sharp contrast to the dribbling game that he'd been brought up on at Harrow, Alcock was responsible for the earliest mention of the term "combination game", in 1874.

The "combination game" was already being developed before then, most notably by the Royal Engineers team that competed in four of the first five FA Cup Finals, but Alcock's recognition of an attacking strategy in which teammates would accompany the dribbler to offer support for a pass higher up the pitch should still be considered revolutionary. While his peers may have sneered at the "Scottish" passing style and concluded that they knew best, Alcock's analytical mind foresaw an amalgamation of the two. He was also honest enough to alter his tactical beliefs when it became clear that passing had a far greater role in successful attacking play than those around him might have foreseen.

Time can too readily blur the impact of those brave enough to shape history. What becomes commonplace can often lose the lustre of its invention and unorthodoxy. That bestows an extra duty on us to recognise those whose legacy continues to permeate long after their passing. Alcock missed out on an honours system that only awarded its first sporting knighthood 19 years after his death. OBEs, CBEs and MBEs were not inaugurated as means of extraordinary recognition until 1917.

Alcock was a man of wealth but of a contrastingly humble character; he is unlikely to have been perturbed by the lack of formal appreciation for his work. He may have even reasoned that football in England would have plotted its meandering course through history without his punctuation. But that would do a disservice to his influence, his courage and his foresight.

And we can make amends. In 2013, the FA commissioned cultural historian Dr Jane Clayton of the International Football Institute at the University of Central Lancashire to carry out a four-month search for the relatives of eight of the game's forefathers to honour them on the 150th anniversary of the organisation's foundation. Clayton found ancestors of Alcock.

On October 21, 2013, a blue plaque was installed at Wembley Stadium with the relatives of six of the men present, unveiled by Sir Trevor Brooking. We can never thank Alcock enough for his service in ensuring the progression of football from minority pursuit to the great sport of ordinary people. But we can make sure that those lucky enough to benefit from his work will never forget it.

Opposite: Commemorative scroll that was presented to Alcock in 1881 in recognition of his work with the Football Association, along with "a silver inkstand and candlesticks".

Above: Alcock (right), pictured alongside the great cricket innovator W.G. Grace, at the Kennington Oval circa 1900.

Below: Unveiling of a commemorative plaque with ancestors of six of the eight men who worked to found the Football Association present, 2013.

CHAPTER TWO

OLYMPIC SUCCESS AND THE GREAT WAR

1900s–1910s

DURING THE FINAL YEARS OF THE 19TH CENTURY, BRITAIN WAS THE LEADER OF WORLD FOOTBALL. THE FA CUP AND SCOTTISH CUP WERE THE TWO OLDEST CUP COMPETITIONS AND ENGLAND'S FOOTBALL LEAGUE WAS THE FIRST DOMESTIC LEAGUE COMPETITION, FORMED IN 1888. SCOTLAND AND IRELAND FOLLOWED SUIT WITH THEIR OWN LEAGUES IN 1890.

But Britain also played a starring role in the game's international expansion. Expatriates, British Empire officials and sailors all spread the gospel of football wherever they travelled to. Visitors to Britain also took the game back to their home countries. In 1891, Argentina became the first country outside Britain to found its own domestic league. Belgium did the same in 1895 followed by Switzerland in 1899. Spain's Copa del Rey was formed in 1901, while Norway established its own domestic cup competition the following year.

In this period, British men and clubs essentially facilitated the formation of modern European football. In Italy, Genoa were set up to represent England abroad, while Englishman Herbert Kilpin founded AC Milan. Brazilian club Corinthians was started as a tribute to the English amateur club of the same name that had toured Brazil so successfully. Scot John Livingstone is regarded as one of the pioneers of football in Chile. Juventus' kit was provided by Notts County, while Barcelona's colours were a replica of the Merchant Taylors' School in Crosby, Liverpool, thanks to two former pupils who were heavily involved during the club's infancy.

As the game expanded internationally, England was cordially invited to be part of it. The Dutch Football Association wrote to the FA in 1902 to extol the virtues of European unity and an international tournament to reflect it, campaigning for the formation of a Fédération Internationale de Football Association (FIFA), but were given short shrift. When the French Football Association sent their own letter a year later, the reply smacked of disinterest and indifference: "The Council of the Football Association cannot see the advantages of such a Federation, but on all matters upon which joint action was desirable they would be prepared to confer."

In part that reflected the English game's insularity. Their view of high-level international football was solely restricted to the British Home Championship and any alternative proposals were viewed as upstarts. England did not play any of these emerging footballing nations until three years after the end of the Great War.

But that insularity was understandable. If England had been dominant in the British Home Championship, thoughts may have turned to seeking out new competition. But between 1896 and 1903, England only won three Championships outright to Scotland's four, and won only two of their eight matches against Scotland. They considered – not unreasonably – that the annual tournament provided enough competition to satisfy supporters and generate improvement in the England team.

So it followed that on May 21, 1904, in a back room of the headquarters of the Union des Sociétés Françaises de Sports Athlétiques in Paris, FIFA was officially formed with France, Belgium, Spain, Sweden, Switzerland, Denmark and the Netherlands its founding members. Its initial intention was not to create an international tournament (although that was an obvious progression) but to formalise laws of the game to be shared across member countries and provide international governance to a quickly growing sport.

Although the FA had not initially declared an interest in this Europe-wide initiative, there were some reservations and regret that England had not led the way. By 1905, the FA had approved FIFA's existence and, a year later, officially joined the organisation. FIFA's recognition of England's role in developing the game and sparking its expansion was honoured by the appointment of Daniel Burley Woolfall – the FA treasurer – to the role of FIFA president, replacing Frenchman Robert Guerin.

With FIFA concerning themselves with governance and the unity of rules, international football's first tournaments came via the nascent modern Olympics. When London hosted the Summer Games in 1908, the Football Association was asked to organise the football competition and also submitted a team in Sweden in 1912.

Although playing under the symbolic banner of Great Britain, the FA picked the squad and in both 1908 and 1912 all players were English and played in the English league, with The National Olympic Committee for Great Britain and Ireland requesting that the Football Association send an English national amateur team in accordance with the 'Olympic spirit'. That clearly favoured England, who had a far better established and richer history of amateur football than their European peers. At the time, many league clubs employed players on professional contracts and those on amateur terms; selection was limited to those who were amateurs. Notable names included Vivian Woodward (Tottenham Hotspur), Harold Hardman (Manchester United) and Arthur Berry (Everton).

England's players excelled in both tournaments, winning both competitions with embarrassing ease and – in the minds of the FA – justifying the previous decision to use the British Home Championship as their sole source of competitive football. In six matches in 1908 and 1912, Great Britain scored 33 goals and conceded just three, never once giving up a lead. It reinforced the inherent supposition within the English game that they were world leaders in the sport.

Although Harry Stapley scored six goals in the 1908 London Olympics and Harry Walden scored nine goals in Stockholm four years later, Woodward was the captain and the undoubted amateur star of English football. Beginning his league career at Tottenham, Woodward didn't become a regular until the age of 23 due to his cricket commitments

and work as an architect and rejected all offers of professional contracts to remain on amateur terms. He briefly retired in 1909 to focus on his work, but was subsequently persuaded to join Chelsea.

Woodward's goalscoring record for England was astonishing. He scored 57 goals in 44 games for the England amateur team and 29 in 23 for the senior England side. His goal total was not beaten until 1958 and his ratio of goals per game will surely never be surpassed.

Back in the British Home Championship, Blackburn Rovers lionheart Bob Crompton became England's linchpin. A defender who excelled at both centre-back and full-back, Crompton captained Rovers to the league title in 1912 and 1914, the latter at the age of 34. His consistency for England was remarkable – between 1906 and 1914, Crompton played in 34 of their 35 matches. Twenty-two of those caps came as captain, a record that wasn't broken until England's greatest captain Billy Wright appeared against Ireland in 1951.

Below: Team photo of the Great Britain side that won the Olympic football tournament in 1908, Shepherd's Bush. All players were English.

"THE COUNCIL OF THE FOOTBALL ASSOCIATION CANNOT SEE THE ADVANTAGES OF SUCH A FEDERATION, BUT ON ALL MATTERS UPON WHICH JOINT ACTION WAS DESIRABLE THEY WOULD BE PREPARED TO CONFER."
THE RESPONSE OF THE FOOTBALL ASSOCIATION TO THE PROPOSAL OF AN INTERNATIONAL GOVERNING BODY

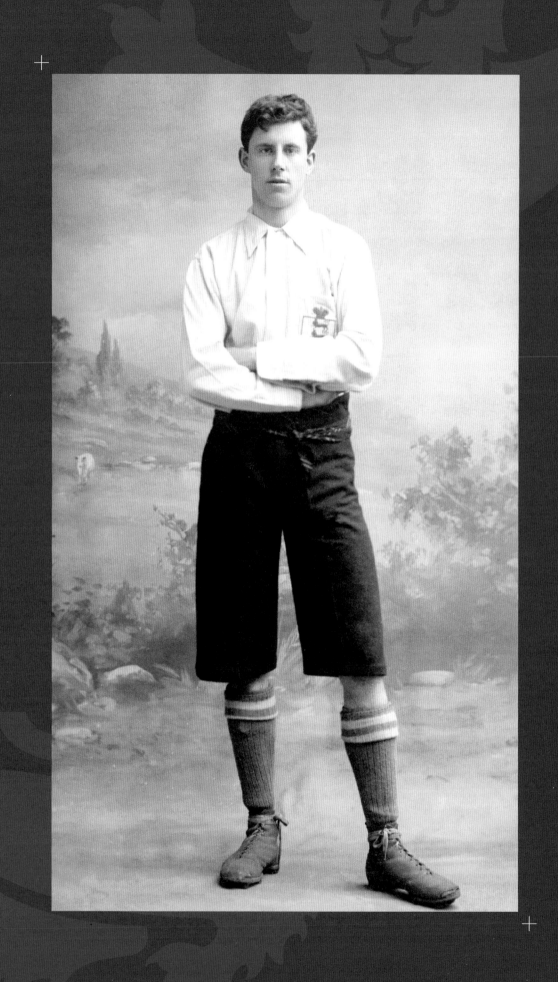

If FIFA's intention was to establish European unity and facilitate expansion into the furthest corners of the world, unity was shattered in 1914 with the outbreak of the Great War. Football immediately found itself in an awkward position. The initial idea was for the leagues to continue as a means of providing a useful distraction from the horrors that filled newspaper front pages and wireless broadcasts. The FA Cup ran its course in 1914–15 despite the British Home Championship being cancelled and the Football League also played on until May 1915. That drew staunch criticism of the FA, most famously from the Dean of Lincoln, who said: ". . .while so many of their fellow men are giving themselves in their country's peril, [supporters] still go gazing at football." Football's reputation suffered post-war for its perceived inaction, deemed unpatriotic in certain quarters.

That seemed more than a little unfair, particularly when the FA itself was criticised. English football's governing body gave extensively to war charities and allowed its headquarters to be used as a storehouse. Matches were used as recruitment drives and grounds became drill centres during the week. By February 1915, it was estimated that football had encouraged half a million men to join the forces.

Football Association president Charles Clegg vocalised the organisation's frustration at the condemnation it had received: "There has been some talk of disgrace being attached to winning the Cup this year, but I do not hold with that opinion… I take the responsibility for the statement that the action which the Football Association took

at the outset would be repeated were the same crisis to arise again… It is sheer twaddle talking about disgrace. The disgrace lay with those who made such a suggestion."

Nevertheless, football could not carry on. It became brutally apparent that the "over by Christmas" predictions of 1914 were wildly over-optimistic and the FA and English clubs understood that their role must pivot to focusing purely on the war effort.

By the time football returned in 1919 and the England national team played together again, the game had given a great service with players, coaches and administrators fighting for their country . Many lives were lost and careers ended by that unspeakably grim conflict. The efforts of the game's forefathers, including, most notably, Charles Alcock and Frederick Wall (who succeeded Alcock as FA secretary), ensured that English football did not need to start again from scratch, but the staunch criticism of 1914 ended football's reputation as "the Gentleman's game". The public, keen to welcome back football after its enforced break, sought greater universality and emotional ownership of their sport.

Opposite: Vivian Woodward, the forward who captained Great Britain to gold medals at the Olympic Games of 1908 and 1912.

Above: Team photo of the Great Britain side that won the gold medal at the 1912 Olympics in Stockholm, Sweden. As in 1908, all were English.

Following pages: England captain Bob Crompton leads the team out at Goodison Park for a match against Scotland, April 1, 1911.

PROFILE:
ENGLAND'S WARTIME HEROES

On September 6, 1914, author Sir Arthur Conan Doyle made a direct appeal for footballers to volunteer for service in the British Army as war began to rage across Europe. With so many players answering the call, a Football Battalion was formed. It was led by Major Frank Buckley, who played for eight clubs in England and was capped by his country against Ireland in 1914.

ajor Buckley later estimated that of the Football Battalion's 600 men, over 500 died. Over 2,000 professional footballers in Britain joined the military service during World War I. On October 21, 2010, the Footballers' Battalion Memorial was unveiled at Longueval, France. It commemorates those who had fought and died in the Great War.

These are merely a selection of the footballers and former footballers who chose to serve their country during each of the two World Wars and lost their lives. Their stories and their service must never be forgotten. They shall grow not old, as we that are left grow old: Age shall not weary them, nor the years condemn. At the going down of the sun and in the morning we will remember them.

Walter Tull was one of English football's first black players and became the British Army's first-ever black officer to command white troops. He played for Clapton, Tottenham Hotspur and Northampton Town between 1908 and 1914. He fought at the Battle of the Somme in 1916 and the Italian Front in 1917 and 1918. On March 25, 1918, Tull was killed during the First Battle of Bapaume. His body was never recovered despite efforts from his comrades to return it to the British position.

Eddie Latheron was a Blackburn Rovers legend who helped them to the league title in 1912 and 1914. Latheron was an exciting inside-forward who earned two caps for England, against Wales in 1913 and Ireland in 1914. After league football ended for the war, Latheron joined the Royal Field Artillery as a gunner. He was killed on October 14, 1917, at the Battle of Passchendaele and is buried at the military cemetery near Ypres in Belgium.

Vivian Woodward scored 29 goals in 23 games for England between 1903 and 1911. Enlisting in the British Army at the outbreak of war in 1914, Woodward was given special dispensation to return to England to play for Chelsea in the FA Cup Final in 1915. However, with teammate Bob Thomson able to play after recovering from injury, Woodward refused to take the place of his friend in the team and returned to war. He was injured by a stray grenade that ended his playing career.

Donald Bell was a gifted amateur footballer with Crystal Palace and Newcastle United who signed professional terms with Bradford Park Avenue in 1912 until war broke out. Bell became the first professional footballer to enlist in the British Army and quickly rose to the role of lance corporal. On July 5, 2016, Bell's actions at the Battle of the Somme, using his own initiative to creep unaided to a communications trench and launching an attack on the enemy, earned him the Victoria Cross for bravery. During a similar display of courage five days later on July 10, 1916, Bell was killed in action.

Evelyn Lintott was a half-back for Plymouth Argyle, Queens Park Rangers, Bradford City and Leeds City, capped seven times by England after turning professional. When war was declared in

Opposite: Walter Tull, one of English football's first black players and the British Army's first black officer to command white troops.

Above right: Vivian Woodward, given special dispensation to return to England from war to play in the FA Cup Final but returned to action. Injured by a stray grenade that ended his career.

Right: Donald Bell, amateur player who was awarded the Victoria Cross for bravery at the Battle of the Somme. Killed in 1916.

 "OVER 2,000 PROFESSIONAL FOOTBALLERS IN BRITAIN JOINED THE MILITARY SERVICE DURING WORLD WAR I." 99

1914, Lintott was one of the first active footballers to enlist. He was promoted to lieutenant and became the first professional footballer to hold a commission. Lintott was one of 19,240 men to lose their lives on July 1, 1916, the first day of the Battle of the Somme.

Tom Cooper played for Port Vale, Derby County and Liverpool, a tough-tackling defender who had a range of passing, unlike many of his peers. He was capped 16 times by England between 1927 and 1934. He would surely have received many more but for a series of injuries that meant he needed cartilage removed from both knees. Cooper enlisted in 1940 and joined the Royal Military Police. He was killed in June 1940 when the dispatch motorcycle he was riding collided with a lorry.

Henry 'Harry' Goslin was a defender who played more than 300 times for Bolton Wanderers, whose entire squad signed up for the army at the outbreak of World War II. Although not listed as an official international, Goslin played four times for England during wartime matches. With war inevitable in 1939, Goslin stood in the centre circle at Burnden Park and informed the crowd that he and his teammates would be enlisting immediately after the match. Goslin was killed in 1943 when a mortar bomb exploded near an observation point that he had set up. He would briefly survive his injuries, but died a few days later.

Herbert 'Herbie' Roberts won four league titles and the FA Cup in Herbert Chapman's great Arsenal team and was capped once by England, against Scotland in 1931. Although Roberts' career was ended by injury in 1937, he enlisted into the Royal Fusiliers in 1939. He served until 1944, when he died from an infection (erysipelas) while on duty. Roberts was one of nine Arsenal players to pass away during their service.

Reginald 'Reg' Anderson was an amateur footballer who played for Dulwich Hamlet and Cardiff City and was given three caps for the England amateur team in 1938 and 1939. Aged only 22 at the outbreak of World War II, he signed up to the Royal Air Force Volunteer Reserve. On the night of February 23, 1942, Anderson was taking part in a minelaying exercise when his plane was shot down over the North Sea. All four crew members were killed when their plane crashed into dunes on the island of Sylt in northern Germany.

Opposite above: Corporal Don Howe and Sergeant Harry Goslin, both of Bolton Wanderers, prepare for an artillery exercise in March 1940. Howe would survive the war, but Goslin would not.

Opposite below: The Footballers' Battalion. Led by Major Frank Buckley, it provided a focal point for football's support of the war effort.

Above: Don Howe and Harry Goslin, part of the Bolton Wanderers squad who signed up en masse to fight in World War II. Killed in 1943 after injuries sustained in a mortar explosion.

CHAPTER THREE

INTRA-WAR YEARS

1920s – 1930s

IT NOW SEEMS UNTHINKABLE THAT THE ORIGINAL WEMBLEY STADIUM, WITH
ITS ICONIC TWIN TOWERS, WAS ORIGINALLY INTENDED TO BE A TEMPORARY
CONSTRUCTION THAT WOULD BE DEMOLISHED. PLANNED TO HOST THE BRITISH
EMPIRE EXHIBITION, THE TONE OF THE PROJECT – AND ITS REPUTATION AMONGST
THE POPULATION – WAS TRANSFORMED BY THE FOOTBALL ASSOCIATION'S DECISION
TO MAKE THE STADIUM THE FA CUP FINAL'S HOME FOR AT LEAST 21 YEARS.

Within weeks, offers of financial support were delivered in a wave of enthusiasm and national pride. The appeal fund became oversubscribed and the architects were able to construct this great tribute to the country's national game.

It was a remarkable feat of architecture and construction: 27,000 tonnes of concrete and steel were assembled at a cost of £750,000. It was without doubt the grandest, mightiest sporting stadium on earth, bigger than Rome's great Colosseum. When a uniformed battalion stomped their boots on the terraces to test the structure and no weakness was detected, Wembley Stadium was complete. It had taken just 300 days to construct, the paint drying only four days before the 1923 FA Cup Final that marked its opening.

Before Wembley, England were a nomadic team. Their seven games directly prior to their first at their new home had taken place across the country in Sheffield, Blackburn, London, West Bromwich, Birmingham, Liverpool and Sunderland. Not only did Wembley provide England with a permanent abode, playing there took on a mythical status.

Above: 'The Stadium Terrace' – photo of Wembley Stadium, taken during the British Empire Exhibition of 1924.

Opposite: Aerial photo of Wembley Stadium and its approach, taken during the British Empire Exhibition of 1924.

England marked the end of the Great War with a series of (technically unofficial) Victory Internationals against Scotland and Wales. These also served as a way of assessing the squad after the effects of a four-year footballing hiatus ahead of the resumption of British Home Championship football.

The conflict had a long-term legacy for the England team. The Football Association not only refused to countenance fixtures against countries who had fought against the Allied powers in the war, but extended that to any country who did agree to such fixtures. FIFA, unsurprisingly given their vision of unity, had a different view. It believed that football should be used to build bridges, even with political enemies.

If that disagreement led to the FA's eventual withdrawal from FIFA in 1920, there was another, more practical reason. FIFA had commenced planning for an international tournament under its own terms that would address the lack of organised international football outside the confines of the Olympics, but believed wholeheartedly in amateur players who competed being financially compensated for their loss of regular earnings. The FA vehemently disagreed, figuring that it would lead to the "shamateurism" that had blighted its early years. This was a trend by which clubs would offer alternative jobs, often in companies connected to the chairman of the club, that were often comparatively highly paid in a bid to attract amateur players to the team.

On the pitch, England had more pressing concerns – the intra-war years were defined by poor performance in the British Home Championship. In fact, England's first game at the new Wembley Stadium was a 1–1 draw with Scotland that saw England finish in last place for the first time in their history. That ended a four-match winless run against Northern Ireland, Belgium, Wales and Scotland that would have been unthinkable two decades earlier.

Between 1919 and 1937, England won only four of the annual British Home Championship tournaments, two fewer than previous also-rans Wales, and four fewer than Scotland, the new dominant force in British football. England won only six of their 20 official games against Scotland between the two wars.

In part, England's failure was down to the alarming turnover of players, an inevitability given the process by which teams were selected. With the 14-man International Select Committee nominating players and then voting on which positions they should take, little thought was given to team balance and harmony. Club loyalty was also a factor. 1924 was the perfect example – 37 different players were used in five matches. Players were drafted in and out, never to be seen on the international stage again. Between 1919 and 1930, a staggering 66 players won a single cap for their country.

England rejoined FIFA in 1924, a sign of warming relations. They faced a select group of opponents over the following years: France

and Belgium regularly and Spain in 1929, against whom they lost their 24-match unbeaten run against foreign opposition. Despite the invitation to take part in the inaugural World Cup in 1930 – and with FIFA doing their best to persuade them – no home nation took part in the tournament as England had again resigned from the organisation in protest at proposed payments for amateur players. The same was true in 1934 and 1938.

Instead, England preferred to arrange matches against other countries that did not participate or were not invited to the World Cup. In 1930, they travelled to Berlin to play Germany in an official match for the first time – where they were surprised by the quality of their opponents in a 3–3 draw – and Vienna, where they drew 0–0 with Austria. By the middle of the decade, Austria were regarded as the best team in Europe.

The pattern continued in 1934, England losing to Hungary and Czechoslovakia in Budapest and Prague respectively. If both defeats were unexpected and pricked the bubble of self-assurance that had long engulfed the England team, better news was to follow in November.

Having skipped the 1934 World Cup, England invited the reigning holders Italy to their first match in London, now infamous as "the Battle of Highbury". With the Italians incensed by a wild tackle from Arsenal's Ted Drake on Luis Monti and having gone 3–0 down, they went on the offensive. Eddie Hapgood had his nose broken, Ray Bowden damaged his ankle, Eric Brook fractured an arm and Drake was punched as

England held on to win 3–2 in an extraordinarily bad-tempered friendly. English pride was restored – they had beaten the world champions.

Still, it was becoming clear – at least in hindsight – that England were wilfully blind to the growing football culture in Continental Europe and South America. Regular fixtures against those opponents – Uruguay, Argentina, Brazil, Italy, Czechoslovakia and Hungary – may have offered a broader assessment of the quality of the England team (and its selection processes) in comparison with their international peers.

But would England have heeded those lessons at the time? Was England a country to take on board chastening defeats and change its own football culture to address the gap? Was the sport organised enough to effect a modern-style root-and-branch review that altered the domestic game to suit the needs of the national team? It seems a little far-fetched to suggest so.

Furthermore, it's not as if England didn't have some remarkably gifted and successful footballers during that period. Dixie Dean, Ted Drake and Cliff Bastin were three of the best attackers in the game in the 1930s. After them came Stanley Matthews and Tommy Lawton; Matthews was named by *France Football* magazine as the inaugural winner of the Ballon d'Or at the age of 41 ahead of Alfredo Di Stefano and Raymond Kopa. In defence, Eddie Hapgood was arguably the best left-back in the world in the 1930s.

And England did respond to their British Home Championship slump. In 1938, they benefited from a shock Scotland defeat to Wales to win the tournament (despite still losing a game to the Scots). A year later, England slipped up against Wales but fought back from a goal down at Hampden Park in front of almost 150,000 supporters to win 2–1 and share the trophy.

Better still was to come in 1938, when England faced a FIFA Select XI to mark the 75th anniversary of the Football Association. The

"…A NASTY BLOW TO OUR PRIDE AND UNDERSTANDING OF WHAT THE GAME WAS ALL ABOUT."

MAURICE EDELSTON OF WIMBLEDON FC ON GREAT BRITAIN'S EXIT FROM THE 1936 OLYMPIC GAMES.

FIFA team was managed by the great Italian coach Vittorio Pozzo and he picked the cream of Europe for the game at Highbury: five Italians (including the great Silvio Piola), two Germans and one player each from France, Belgium, Hungary and Norway. England swept away their opponents 3–0.

Even so, there was some evidence that England were falling behind the world's best. When England beat Austria 4–3 in 1932, spectators (and England's players) were surprised by the effectiveness, accuracy and forethought of the Austrians' passing and their speed of transition from defence to attack. England had been favourites due to conditions and their home advantage, but rode their luck and there was some dismay that the home team had not dominated play.

Opposite above: Austrian team enters the field of play ahead of their fixture against England at Stamford Bridge, December 1932.

Opposite below: Crowds gather outside Chelsea's Stamford Bridge, awaiting entry to watch England vs Austria, December 1932.

Above: Austrian squad training before facing England in 1932.

Opposite: Everton teammates Dixie Dean (left) and Tommy Johnson
pose ahead of an England international, March 4, 1931.

Above: The captains of England and Italy shake hands before their
ill-tempered friendly at Highbury in November 1934.

Below: Match action from England vs Italy in November 1934.
England won a highly physical match 3–2.

By 1936, that suspicion had spread to the players themselves. When a slightly patched-up Great Britain squad (with 10 of the 15 spaces given to English amateur players) struggled past China and were eliminated by Poland at the Berlin Olympic Games, Maurice Edelston of Wimbledon FC remarked that the tournament had been "a nasty blow to our pride and understanding of what the game was all about".

And then Austria had their revenge at the sixth attempt. Hugo Meisl's "Wunderteam" hosted England in Vienna and beat the visitors 2–1, assisted by the brilliance of captain Walter Nausch, Josef Bican and Matthias Sindelar, who could probably claim to be the best player in the world. This time, it was England who were reassured that they had *only* lost by a small margin.

It's easy to say that England made a mistake in not participating in the first three World Cups. Not only did it stop them observing (and improving against) the most capable teams in the world in a competitive environment, but they might well have won at least one of those tournaments. Their victory in 1934 over champions Italy (who were motivated to win the match by Benito Mussolini's promise of an Alfa Romeo for each player if they managed it) suggests as much, as did the success over the FIFA Select XI.

Had England known that the World Cup would become a showpiece event in the global sporting calendar, they may well have changed their minds. It is not entirely fanciful to suggest that England might be behind only Germany, Brazil and Italy with three Jules Rimet Trophies. But by the time England were ready to participate, the world went to war again.

Above: Italian team posing for a photo in 1934. On the far left is Vittorio Pozzo, a brilliant manager and tactical innovator.

Right: A young Stanley Matthews, who made his England debut against Wales in 1934.

Opposite: The Duke of Connaught meets the Italian players before their game against England in 1934. Shaking his hand is winger Raimundo Orsi.

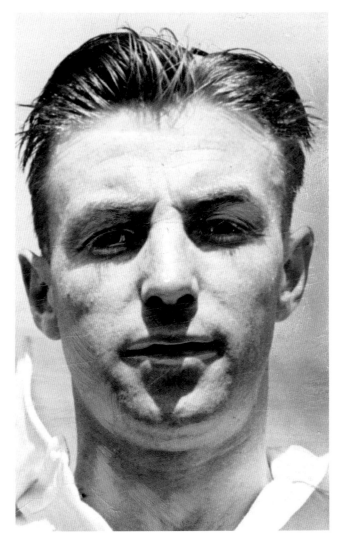

CHAPTER FOUR

FOUNDATIONS
FOR THE FUTURE

1940s

THE FIRST CHALLENGE WAS ENSURING THE MATCH COULD EVEN TAKE PLACE. WITH A RECORD CROWD DESPERATE TO WITNESS THE RETURN OF INTERNATIONAL FOOTBALL, SUPPORTERS CROUCHED BY THE TOUCHLINE AND BEHIND THE GOAL AS REFEREE WILLIE WEBB PLEADED WITH THEM TO MOVE BACK AND GIVE THE PLAYERS SOME SPACE. AFTER A DELAY, ENGLAND'S PLAYERS JOGGED THROUGH A THRONG OF BODIES AND ENTERED THE PITCH. IN 1939, 36,000 PEOPLE WATCHED NORTHERN IRELAND HOST ENGLAND AT WINDSOR PARK. IN 1946, THE EXACT ATTENDANCE WAS CALCULATED AT 57,111.

From the kick-off, George Hardwick was able to advance with the ball and sent a hopeful cross into the box. Northern Irish defender Tom Aherne misjudged his clearance, the ball skewing off his boot, allowing Raich Carter to pounce. England's players had waited seven and a half years to resume their international careers; they had needed less than a minute to celebrate their return.

English football enjoyed a tremendous boom in the years immediately following World War II. There was a widespread recognition of the role played by the sport in contributing to the war effort. The Football Association had cooperated with bodies including the Red Cross, the War Office and Civil Defence. Players and coaches had helped prepare soldiers physically for the rigours of combat. Football grounds across the country had become Fitness for Service centres and the FA had made significant donations to war charities.

And football had helped to maintain the mood during wartime, when the game had temporarily paused its obsession with the pursuit of victory and silverware to return to the principles that underpinned its popularity – exercise, mutual respect, friendly competition and team unity. To make up the numbers, guest players were parachuted in, and professionals were picked alongside part-timers, youngsters and even members of the public.

That spirit, that notion of football as a force for unity and morale, continued into peacetime. Thousands of men who had lost six years of their lives to war, and families who had suffered unspeakable loss, saw football as an antidote to the often brutal reality of post-war rebuilding. War had, finally, provoked lasting peace, but it hardly provoked an immediate return to well-being for many. The national sport played a role in escapism and distraction and the public warmly welcomed its presence. By 1948–49, cumulative attendances for league football hit a peak of 41.3 million.

The end of World War II also caused an understandable shift in England's relationship with FIFA. Although arguments over "broken time" payments – the compensation of players for expenses and missed time from their employers – and the true meaning of amateurism lingered on, the FA understood the need for European unity and rejoined FIFA after a series of meetings at the end of the conflict. Any reservations over a difference in ideals were rendered insignificant, with harmony the only end goal. Never again would England sit outside of the sport's world governing body.

FIFA had always craved British involvement in its structure; for all the rapid globalisation of the sport, Britain was still its natural home at that time. And with FIFA suffering a considerable financial headache due to the lack of international sport during the war years, the FA believed it could assist. A fixture between a Great Britain XI and the Rest of Europe was organised for May 1947 and raised £34,000 for FIFA, largely thanks to an attendance of 134,000 at Hampden Park. It served the FA well to remind the wider game of its draw and its formidable strength (the British XI won 6–1); it served FIFA well because the proceeds effectively guaranteed its economic future.

If the 1940s were defined by the resurgence of domestic football in post-war England and the displays of unity between the FA and FIFA, the England team were also looking to the future. In 1946, and before England travelled to Windsor Park, Walter Winterbottom was officially announced as the first-ever manager of the national team (his initial role would be Director of Coaching).

The innovation of his appointment can be viewed best through the widespread criticism it received. Winterbottom believed in the

Opposite: Match action from Great Britain vs the Rest of Europe at Hampden Park in May 1947. The game was watched by 134,000 spectators.

"THE CLOSEST TO PERFECTION I EVER SAW ON A FOOTBALL FIELD."

BILLY WRIGHT ON ENGLAND'S 10–0 THRASHING OF PORTUGAL.

power of coaching, both as a means of improving individual players and the standard of play across the country, but others vehemently disagreed. "Unless this coaching monster is seized firmly by the throat it will strangle the living grace out of our game," one former England international said. "He believes too much in words and diagrams."

Winterbottom did not have everything his own way. He was still forced to pick the team through a selection committee. His attempts to introduce pre-match training sessions and player meetings in which squad members were invited to openly discuss tactics were initially viewed – at least by outsiders – with a mix of suspicion and derision. But he believed in the method.

Winterbottom's role would not have worked – or even got off the ground – without the determination of Stanley Rous above him. Rous had immersed himself in English football during the 1930s, refereeing the 1934 FA Cup Final before rewriting the Laws of the Game in 1938. He served as secretary of the Football Association for 28 years until 1962.

Rous had been instrumental in the return of the home nations to FIFA and was determined to give the FA and English football far greater organisation and thus cohesion. His grand intention – with Winterbottom's appointment one stage in it – was to create a firm structure for the national game that tied together every level of football in England: grassroots, amateur clubs, professional clubs and the national team set-up.

That reflected not only Rous's hope that England could exert its influence as the birthplace of the modern game, but his insistence that arrogance should not blind anyone to the need for constant improvement. It was he, more than anyone, who aimed to destroy the myth that England could always consider itself as one of the pillars of world football simply "because we're England".

Whether Rous and Winterbottom can take all the credit for England's immediate post-war form is open to debate, but there's no doubt that England re-established themselves as the dominant force in the home nations and were astonishingly prolific as they broadened their horizons to new European opponents. Between the end of World War II and the 1950 World Cup, England won 22 of their 29 matches and scored four or more goals in 13 of them.

The headline victories came against Portugal (whom England faced for the first time in 1947) and Italy in 1948. In Lisbon, England overcame their disappointment at losing to Switzerland a week earlier by thrashing the Portuguese 10–0, a match Billy Wright described as "the closest to perfection I ever saw on a football field".

A year later, reigning world champions Italy hosted England at the Stadio Comunale in Turin and the visitors produced one of the most remarkable victories in their history. Seven of the Italian side were

Opposite: Match action shots from Great Britain's victory over the Rest of Europe in May 1947.

Above: Stanley Rous, who served as secretary of the Football Association for 28 years until 1962.

selected from the great Torino team that had won three Serie A titles in succession and were playing at their home stadium. But they were dismantled by an England team that played attacking, aesthetically wonderful football. The 4–0 win was – not unreasonably – viewed back home as proof that England were the best team in the world if they performed at their best.

In the British Home Championship, England were just as dominant. Between 1946 and 1961, they either won outright or shared the win in 13 of 15 years (the tournament was decided by points only, rather than goal difference or head-to-head records as separators. There was a pattern to England's results in the 1940s: tense, tight matches against Scotland, spectacular wins over Northern Ireland (including a 9–2,

Opposite: Stanley Matthews works on his tactical knowledge with a game of Subbuteo against England teammate Stan Mortensen.

Above: Stanley Matthews in action for England. Matthews was named as the first European Footballer of the Year in 1956.

Below: Matthews shaking the hand of Prime Minister Clement Attlee before England played Belgium on January 19, 1946.

7–2 and a 6–2), and ruthless efficiency against Wales, against whom they conceded only once in four matches.

Although there were no major tournaments in the 1940s for England to showcase their abilities, it's abundantly clear that this was a golden age for the Three Lions. If World War II had robbed several players of the chance to establish themselves on the international stage (Tommy Lawton was the only player to feature in England's last match before the conflict and the first after it), in the immediate post-war years Winterbottom was able to call upon many who could legitimately be considered amongst the best in their position in the world.

In goal, Frank Swift turned 30 three years before the end of the war but still established himself as an ultra-reliable goalkeeper, and only retired in 1949. George Hardwick was forced to retire in 1948 with a knee injury, but was a prodigious left-back who is recognised as Middlesbrough's greatest-ever defender and the only player from the club to captain his country. In central defence, Billy Wright made his debut in England's first post-war game in Belfast and first captained his country in the 6–2 victory over the same opponents in 1948.

But it was England's forward line that was the envy of Europe. With Winterbottom setting England up in the W-M formation that was de rigueur at the time, England's manager had Tom Finney and Stanley Matthews as the outside-left and outside-right respectively; their dribbling was worth the meagre entrance fee alone. The inside-left and inside-right positions, slightly deeper and more central roles, were typically filled by Wilf Mannion and Stan Mortensen, who both reached 25 caps, with Mortensen managing 23 goals. The centre-forward role was typically trusted to Tommy Lawton and his brilliant heading, or the great Newcastle United forward Jackie Milburn.

Pushing for a place were a number of other talented attackers who, in any other era, might well have been staples of the England team. Len Shackleton was one of English football's great entertainers, whose skill on the ball was deemed second to none. Stan Pearson

scored five hat-tricks for Manchester United, including their first-ever against Liverpool. Jack Rowley was a teammate of Pearson and is one of only four players to score 200 goals for Manchester United. Bobby Langton was a brilliant outside-left who played for Blackburn, Preston and Bolton in the North West. Jimmy Mullen's goals led Wolverhampton Wanderers to three First Division titles and the FA Cup. That those five players only played 42 times for England between them is proof of England's strength in depth in attacking positions.

Even if the 1940s contained only British Home Championship success with no other major tournament on which to hang their hat, England had good reason to feel bullish about their quality. Landmark victories over Italy had offered clear evidence that England's failure to participate in inaugural World Cups had cost them a chance of multiple honours before war brought football to a halt.

But the chance to put the record straight lay just around the corner. The 1949 British Home Championship also acted as qualification for the 1950 World Cup in Brazil the following summer; England won all three matches, scoring 14 goals and conceding just three. Two of those were in the 9–2 win over Northern Ireland.

Having avoided hosts Brazil, well-fancied Uruguay and holders Italy in the group-stage draw on May 22, England were expected to breeze through a group containing Spain, a Chile team that had failed to even reach the final four of the 1949 South American Championship, and minnows the USA. Expectations were understandably high and the national press believed that bringing the Jules Rimet Trophy to England was a near certainty. This was England's overdue opportunity to stamp their authority on the international stage.

Opposite: Stanley Rous helps to conduct an FA Cup draw in 1946.

Above, from left: Portrait and match action shot of Tom Finney, who temporarily became England's record goalscorer and won 76 caps for his country.

SIR WALTER WINTERBOTTOM

It was too much to ask for Walter Winterbottom's management of England to be an unqualified success. He had done so much for so many to shape the future of the English game and its national team that there had to be a flaw. For Winterbottom, that flaw was World Cup football. England crashed out in 1950 and never got beyond the quarter-finals in his four attempts to achieve sporting immortality. Against the high expectations and melodrama of the pre-tournament media circus, Winterbottom fell short.

Winterbottom's explanation, although he never publicly sought excuses, might have been that you can take a national sport to water but cannot make it drink. He operated under suspicion and doubt, perennially fighting against the tide. His teams were picked by other people, his ideas picked apart by a great many more. If a team can only realise its potential when every element points in the same direction, Winterbottom never enjoyed that luxury.

Born in Oldham in 1913, a year before the outbreak of the Great War, Winterbottom became an amateur player before signing professional terms with Manchester United. Forever wondering what might be around the corner, he used his salary to train as a teacher. It proved an invaluable decision when a spinal disease forced him to retire from playing at the age of just 25.

Winterbottom's second chance in the game came due to the timing of World War II. Having joined the Royal Air Force, he was appointed as the chief instructor of physical training at RAF Cosford and then the Air Ministry. Turning out as an occasional guest player for Chelsea, Winterbottom was asked to run coaching courses on behalf of the FA at various London schools. Stanley Rous, by then secretary of the FA, was impressed.

Rous, himself a visionary in terms of how football should be organised and taught, persuaded the FA Council to create a new role for Winterbottom. Not only would he be the FA's first Director of Coaching, he would also be the first England team manager.

Winterbottom is still England's youngest-ever manager and their longest-serving, but the title is a little misleading given the modern responsibilities of the role. England's team continued to be picked by a selection committee until Winterbottom persuaded them otherwise when his replacement Alf Ramsey was appointed in 1962.

Although Rous was the driver behind Winterbottom's appointment, fitting seamlessly into the culture around him was always going to be difficult. Winterbottom felt it necessary to take elocution lessons to smooth off the edges of his Lancastrian accent in order to be taken seriously. If many of English football's most successful clubs were based in the Midlands and the North, the governance of the game was still overwhelmingly southern and upper class. Winterbottom was comparatively young and the son of a ring frame fitter in a textile factory.

Winterbottom's grand design was not just to create a high-performing England team but to revolutionise the coaching systems and methods across the nation, creating a sustainable framework that would identify and improve talented players. He formed the national coaching scheme with residential courses at Lilleshall in Shropshire. To give the courses greater authority, he persuaded members of his squad to enrol and then take exams to achieve FA coaching badges.

Opposite: Walter Winterbottom (1913–2002), the first manager of the England football team.

Below: Walter Winterbottom takes a training session with the England team in 1961.

-65

We need only to look at the list of young coaches that Winterbottom surrounded himself with (and mentored) for proof of his extensive influence: Bill Nicholson, Ron Greenwood, Malcolm Allison, Joe Mercer, Vic Buckingham, Don Howe, Bobby Robson. Three of those men managed England and they won nine league titles between them. More significantly, four of the seven worked abroad, often with great success. That is proof that Winterbottom's methods were deliberately expansive, breaking away from the isolationism that had often hampered English coaches.

If Winterbottom revelled in his role as a pioneer, his management of the England team was far more difficult. He craved control over team selection before, true to form, earning the right for his successor. He faced prejudice for his lack of experience of the professional game and his revolutionary ideas about training, match preparation and nutrition were met with resistance by some senior players who had grown up on the principles of hard work and physical fitness. Winterbottom paid a price for thinking ahead of his time.

If England were humbled in the 1950s under Winterbottom's watch, against the USA, Chile, Uruguay, Hungary and the USSR, it was not because their manager was complacent or blind to the threat. He repeatedly warned of the dangers of football's growth in South America and Continental Europe, particularly before the first fateful game against Hungary in 1953.

Perhaps Winterbottom lacked the dictatorial edge that his players of the time required, and his successor Alf Ramsey certainly provided that to memorable effect. Maybe his remit was simply too great, giving him absolute responsibility without absolute power.

We must judge Winterbottom by the legacy he left for those who followed him and those whose task was made easier by his work. He truly revolutionised the coaching of football in England, establishing pathways to the senior team by creating youth squads and a 'B' team. And he dealt with the slings and arrows with unshakeable humility.

In some ways English football was dogged by the insularity that enveloped its society in the early decades of the 20th century. But nobody fought against them more than Winterbottom and Rous, his greatest confidant. If Ramsey provided the strength of personality and discipline to haul England over the line in 1966, the foundations of that great national triumph were laid before his time. It is no exaggeration to call Winterbottom the father of modern English football.

Opposite, clockwise from top: Winterbottom directing training; bust of Winterbottom, unveiled at St George's Park in 2013; at London Airport before flying to Chile for the 1962 World Cup.

Above: Winterbottom and the England squad arrive back at London Airport following their shock defeat to the United States at the 1950 World Cup.

CHAPTER FIVE

CHASTENING DEFEATS

1950s

IT WAS THE BIGGEST SHOCK IN WORLD CUP HISTORY. IT WAS THE MOST DISMAL DEFEAT IN THE STORIED SAGA OF ENGLISH SPORT. IT WAS AN UPSET SO REMARKABLE THAT MANY BRITISH NEWSPAPERS ASSUMED THAT THERE HAD BEEN A MISTAKE DOWN THE WIRES; ENGLAND HAD SURELY WON 10–1, NOT LOST 1–0. *THE NEW YORK TIMES* BELIEVED THEY WERE THE VICTIMS OF AN ELABORATE HOAX AND DELAYED REPORTING THE SCORE. BUT THERE IT STAYED, A STATUE TO SPORTING HUMILIATION: ENGLAND 0–1 USA. TIME CAN SOFTEN THE EDGES OF EMBARRASSMENT, BUT NOTHING CAN CHANGE THE SCORELINE.

The American team that faced England in Belo Horizonte on June 29, 1950, was a collection of part-timers. It included a Scottish player released by Wrexham, a Haitian centre-forward (who scored the winner) and, most famously, a baseball catcher who had been converted into a goalkeeper. The USA were made 500–1 outsiders in a two-team contest, and few punters scrambled to take advantage.

England, competing in their first World Cup, were beaten not just by their opponents but some astonishing bad luck. Reports estimate that Walter Winterbottom's team enjoyed more than 90 per cent possession and hit the woodwork no fewer than 11 times. And after the USA had been rescued by the umpteenth last-ditch tackle, improbable save, questionable refereeing decision or fortuitous deflection, England must have felt like they were taking on fate itself, against which they had no answer.

"Very reluctantly I left my seat and made my way to the England dressing room," Stanley Matthews later recalled. "I wouldn't like to describe what I met there, so I will draw a veil over it. It was a disaster. If we'd played for 24 hours we wouldn't have scored. It was one of those days."

The media reaction – beyond simple disbelief – was predictably scathing. The Daily Herald mimicked the famous Sporting Times notice of 1882: a mock obituary that led to cricket's Ashes series: "In affectionate remembrance of English Football, which died in Rio on 2 July, 1950. Duly lamented by a large circle of sorrowing friends and acquaintances. RIP. NB: The body will be cremated and the ashes taken to Spain."

If England's humiliation had required a double dose of misfortune, it was partly born out of a lack of preparation. Given that Brazil was their opportunity to lay down a marker after choosing to sidestep the first three World Cups, England made things unnecessarily difficult for themselves.

The party travelled late to South America as an acclimatisation period was deemed too costly. They stayed in a hotel that lacked air conditioning and which provided catering services that left players "feeling sick". The squad complained of the effects of heat and humidity after 45 minutes of their opening-match victory over Chile and were robbed of sleep by firecrackers set off outside the hotel.

England sent Arthur Drewry – a member of the selection committee – to Brazil ahead of the players and allowed him to shape team selection. They sent Stanley Matthews on a goodwill tour of Canada, meaning that he joined up with his teammates late. None of these are valid excuses for losing to the USA, but they offer part-explanations for their group-stage exit.

The 1950 World Cup provided a wake-up call to English football. At the FA, Stanley Rous created a technical sub-committee charged with consulting stakeholders in the game (including directors, managers, current and former players) for their thoughts on a number of issues including tactics, match preparation, training, the development of young players and refereeing. They received a variety of answers, some including pointed criticism, but that made consensus on a framework for moving forward difficult.

Significant change was shelved for two distinct reasons. Firstly, there was a belief that the main reason for England's capitulation in Brazil was bad luck – not an unreasonable conclusion despite two defeats in three matches. Had they beaten the USA by a deserved margin then they would have beaten Spain too, this theory went. That

Opposite: The USA's Joe Gaetjens scores the winning goal past England goalkeeper Bert Williams to give his side a shock lead that they would not relinquish.

Above, top: Billy Wright and USA captain Ed McIlvenny (right) exchange souvenirs before their World Cup match in Belo Horizonte, Brazil.

Above: Tom Finney tries to head the ball between two American defenders as England struggle to make a breakthrough despite dominating the match throughout.

would have left England as one of the final four alongside Sweden, Brazil and Uruguay, a satisfactory result from a long voyage for their first tournament experience outside of Europe.

And England's fortunes also improved immediately post-World Cup, offering succour for those who believed 1950 was merely a blip. England played 18 official matches between July 1950 and April 1953, losing only once.

After draws against strong European sides France and Yugoslavia, England also drew 1–1 with Italy in Turin, beat Argentina, Portugal, Belgium and Switzerland and were the dominant force in the British Home Championship. On a tour of South America in May 1953, England beat Chile, got their revenge on the USA with a 6–3 win and lost 2–1 to Uruguay in Montevideo despite several members of a small squad suffering from food poisoning.

But 1953 proved a chastening year for England, enough to stamp firmly on the green shoots of recovery witnessed post-Brazil. On October 21, England hosted a Rest of Europe XI at Wembley in front of 96,000 spectators to mark the Football Association's 90th anniversary. Despite their opponents not sharing a common language and being thrust together in the weeks before the match, England were outplayed and outpassed for long periods and were fortunate to earn a 4–4 draw thanks to an 89th-minute Alf Ramsey penalty. Worse was to come in the same stadium the following month.

If Hungary were the mysterious outsiders of European football (they did not enter the 1950 World Cup), there was an increasing body of evidence to suggest that Gusztáv Sebes's team were potentially the best team on the Continent. Their (nominally amateur) team had won the 1952 Olympic football competition and arrived at Wembley having lost just one of their previous 25 matches, a run that eventually extended through to 1956. Sebes used a 2-3-3-2 formation that maximised the brilliance of inside-forwards Sándor Kocsis and Ferenc Puskás by using Nándor Hidegkuti in an innovative free role despite starting as the centre-forward.

England sent a scouting team (an unusual move for the FA at the time) to watch Hungary play Sweden but witnessed a 2–2 draw that tempered concerns about the strength of their forthcoming opponents, not least in the national media. The *Daily Mail* was particularly confident, predicting that England would "finish two or three goals to the good".

From the outset, England were bamboozled by the Hungarians' attacking play. Their forwards interchanged positions, moving into space and creating time on the ball that England's defenders rushed to try and solve. In *The Times*, Geoffrey Green wrote his famous line about Billy Wright trying to tackle Puskás and resembling "a fire engine going in the wrong direction for a blaze", but Wright was not alone.

It was not merely the tactical wizardry that outfoxed England. Hungary's players had a technical ability that left England grasping

Above: Hungary's 'Mighty Magyars' line up before kick-off against England at Wembley in November 1953.

Opposite, clockwise from top left: Ferenc Puskas (No. 10) celebrates scoring Hungary's third goal at Wembley; Puskas and Billy Wright swap pennants before kick-off at Wembley Stadium; and England goalkeeper Gil Merrick tips a shot around the post.

at thin air. Hidegkuti played a series of dummies that were otherwordly, Puskás and Zoltán Czibor second-guessed the movement of one another as if they had practised every day together since they had learned to walk. Tom Finney, injured and watching on alongside 100,000 transfixed supporters in England's national stadium, said it best: "This was the nearest thing to telepathy on a football field, and I doubt if its like will ever be reproduced again in my lifetime."

How about six months later? In the aftermath of the first defeat, the FA set up committees to work towards a greater unity between clubs and the national team to allow Winterbottom to spend more time with players and implement his training ideas. But any extensive autopsy would take far longer than time allowed, and England must have travelled to Budapest with a sense of trepidation. Several newspapers, most notably the *Daily Mail*, predicted that England were set on revenge that might worry their hosts, but even they seemed more hopeful than expectant.

The return game was no less humiliating. Afterwards, Puskás expressed his surprise that England had not altered their shape or apparent strategy from the first game, and his team took England apart. Hungary were 6–0 up within an hour and could feasibly have inflicted a heavier defeat than the final 7–1 scoreline. On the touchline, Winterbottom buried his head in his hands. In the space of four matches, England had suffered their first-ever home defeat to non-British opposition at Wembley and their heaviest-ever loss, a margin of defeat that still stands to this day.

Those two defeats did, finally, signal a change in England's approach. It was widely acknowledged back home that the Hungarians had a method of training and match preparation that relied upon scientific principles, modern equipment and tactical innovation that were shared by many of their Continental peers but not England. Across the country, managers began to appreciate the benefits of technique training that replaced some aspects of their fitness-first approach, something Winterbottom had long campaigned for.

To some extent, pride was restored over the course of the rest of the decade. England were drawn into a tricky group at the 1954 World Cup, but the competition seedings meant that they avoided playing Italy. A win and a draw against Switzerland and Belgium were enough to progress through to the quarter-finals, where they were eliminated 4–2 by Uruguay. Not only was that deemed to be adequate progress after the debacle in Brazil, it also meant England did not have to face Hungary for the third time in a year in the semi-finals.

In Sweden in 1958, England were handed a nightmarish task when drawn together with the USSR (who were rapidly growing in competitive strength), Austria and Brazil. Winterbottom's side earned creditable draws with all three nations but were eliminated after a play-off against the USSR.

A group-stage exit would usually result in serious fallout but England had been hampered by misfortune and tragedy. Tom Finney had been forced out of the tournament after the opening group game and England understandably cried foul about a series of refereeing decisions in their final draw against Austria, which included a nonsensical disallowed goal for an alleged handball. Had England won that game, they would have faced hosts Sweden in the quarter-finals.

Of greater national significance were the grim events of February 6, 1958, when Manchester United's plane crashed on the runway of Munich-Riem Airport having stopped to refuel on their return from a European Cup tie in Belgrade. Nothing could ever overshadow the losses suffered by Manchester United on that terrible night, but England would surely have selected Tommy Taylor, Roger Byrne and Duncan Edwards for their squad, all of whom lost their lives. Bobby Charlton was determined to play a part in Sweden, but was understandably deeply affected by the tragedy.

By the end of the decade, the old guard of England had stepped aside. Between 1957 and 1959, Stanley Matthews, Tom Finney, Nat Lofthouse and Billy Wright all made their final appearances for their

Left: Action from England's 4–2 defeat to Uruguay at the 1954 World Cup.

Below: Wreckage from the plane in the aftermath of the Munich air disaster, which tragically took the lives of 23 people.

Opposite: Bobby Charlton recovers in hospital after sustaining injuries in the crash.

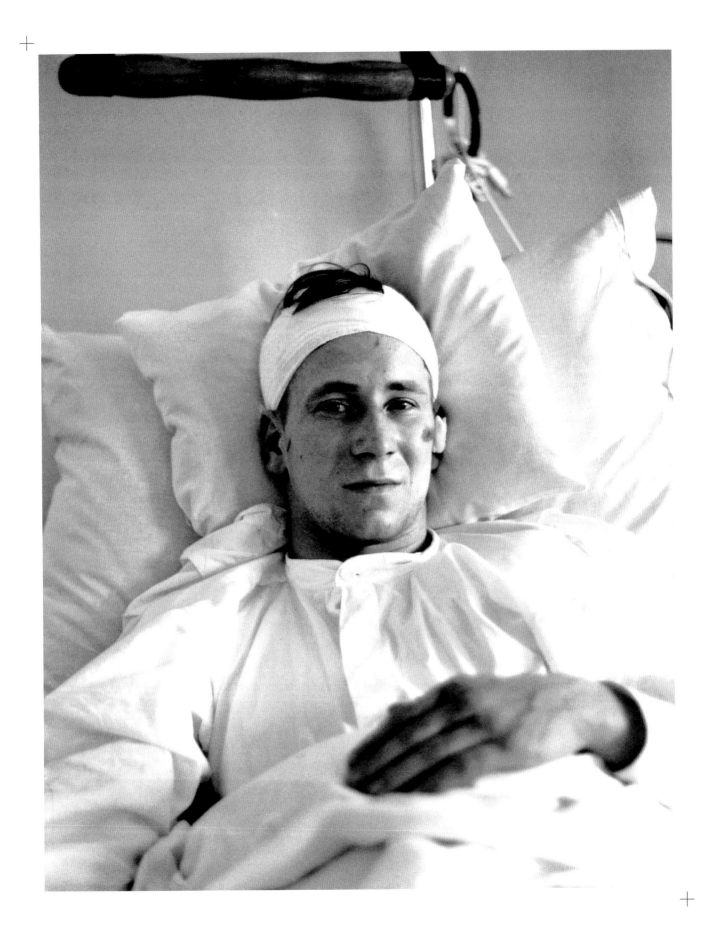

"BUT IN TEAM PLAY WE ARE WAY BEHIND. I'M STILL BEING PREVENTED FROM BUILDING A TEAM. FROM MATCH TO MATCH, THERE ARE TOO MANY CHANGES TO MAKE PLANNING POSSIBLE."

WALTER WINTERBOTTOM ON HIS TIME IN CHARGE OF THE ENGLAND NATIONAL TEAM.

country and England chose to turn to the future rather than fill their positions with stopgaps. Of the 22 players initially named in the 1958 World Cup squad (Alan Hodgkinson and Maurice Setters did not eventually travel), exactly half were aged 23 or under. At the 1954 World Cup, only four had been at that age (and two of those did not travel).

For England's national team, the 1950s were characterised by the repeated cycle of major tournament disappointment that was immediately followed by promising victories that provided hope of better times to come. At each World Cup there were reasons to conclude that England had suffered undue levels of misfortune but also had allowed bad luck to rush into the gap created by complacency.

Walter Winterbottom understood that more than most. By 1953 came his realisation – or perhaps just public expression of his long-held realisation – that his job was becoming impossible. Integral to that suspicion was the ongoing use of the selection committee.

"Some good players are coming through," Winterbottom said. "But in team play we are way behind. I'm still being prevented from building a team. From match to match, there are too many changes to make planning possible."

Another feature of Winterbottom's tenure was that he was overburdened, having been given the responsibility for arranging team travel and hotels, organising training plans ahead of major tournaments and even, on one occasion, asked to miss a scouting trip to arrange medical treatment for one of the selection committee. And that was combined with him lacking the ultimate power to pick – and therefore train and prepare – his own team.

It became clear that change would have to come, not just in the average age of the squad, a new manager or a shift in training (although all three would eventually happen), but in the relationship between clubs and the national team, and the manner in which the business of the England team was organised and carried out. The 1960s would be English football's age of enlightenment. It would bring with it our greatest day.

Opposite: Bobby Charlton and Tom Finney carry Billy Wright in some training ground japes.

Right, from top: Captains Bellini of Brazil and Wright of England shake hands before their World Cup match in 1958; Brazil's Mazzola and England's Don Howe collide during their match in Gothenburg; and match action from a game that ended 0-0.

PROFILE:
BILLY WRIGHT

If Billy Wright's career became a study of triumph through perseverance and hard work, it got off to a fitting start. In 1938, At the age of 14, Wright was given an eight-month trial by Wolverhampton Wanderers manager Major Frank Buckley, but was deemed too small to make the grade. Wolves' trainer Jack Davies had been so impressed with Wright's commitment to removing weeds from the pitch that he requested Wright be kept on to help the ground staff. A decade later, Wright was captaining his country at Wembley.

right became used to dealing with setbacks and roadblocks. Having made his debut for Wolves in 1939, the outbreak of war limited his appearances and he suffered a bad ankle break in 1942 that threatened to end his career before it had really begun. Wright fought back from the injury, became a physical instructor in the army and played matches whenever time allowed.

In Major Buckley's defence, he was right. Wright did indeed lack the physical presence of those around him, particularly in his position at centre half. Although his leap to head the ball bought him a few inches, strikers would feel confident of knocking him off the ball. But he counteracted that physical deficiency with a monastic dedication to his fitness and an ability to read the game that was unmatched during his 13 years as an England player. If the cliché of brains over brawn was made for anyone, it was Wright.

Wright was not a natural choice to be England's captain. His authority was a deliberately quiet one. There were no chest-beating displays of passion or stirring calls to arms that may have better reflected a culture still rooted in military analogy after the end of two World Wars.

But Wright found a different way, a better way. He was inspirational by example on and off the pitch, always available to offer sage advice and generous with his time. His daughter fondly recalls how people would often knock on the door with their young child, desperate to introduce them to the great Billy Wright. More often than not, Wright would invite them in and send them away with one of his England caps. When his wife chided him for such generosity, the reply was always the same: "Don't be daft, I've got loads of them."

When a situation demanded criticism, it would be delivered by Wright with a quiet constructive word rather than bawled at the top of his voice using coarse language.

Opposite: Billy Wright practises his ball control in November 1955. He would become the first man to reach 100 caps for any national team.

Above: Portrait of Wright in his England kit, thought to be in 1955. He would eventually retire from playing in 1959.

Below: Wright shakes the hand of Brazil captain Nilton Santos before a game between the two nations at Wembley Stadium in May 1956.

"I decided early on that captaincy is the art of leadership, not dictatorship," Wright said later. "Respect is the hardest thing for a captain to come by and the easiest to lose. I never changed my mind about this."

That dignified, quiet authority could easily have been mistranslated as timidity or introversion. But none of Wright's teammates were ever left in any doubt about his desire to win. That determination was based partly in a fierce pride in the honour of being asked to lead his country's national team in the years immediately after such a gruelling conflict, but also in the simple wish to be the best footballer, best captain and best role model he could be. Nobody who played with or under Wright had the slightest doubt that he had their back.

To reminisce now on Wright's career is to remember a sepia-tinted age of gentlemen footballers. That shift to the modern age was partly caused by Wright and his marriage to pop star Joy Beverley in July 1958. The pair met when the Beverley Sisters were performing at the Wolverhampton Grand Theatre and fell in love instantly. If being part of a celebrity couple suggested that Wright enjoyed a life in the spotlight, he sidestepped those trappings of fame adroitly. If he was a celebrity, it was never by choice. If he was a gentleman footballer, it was because he had the charm and kindness of a true gent.

Perhaps that warmth of spirit ultimately played against Wright. After retiring, he seemed the ideal candidate to be a manager and was appointed by Arsenal in 1962, three years after his final England appearance. Wright lasted four seasons, but never really suggested that he was making progress. Writer Brian Glanville suggested that Wright "had neither the guile nor the authority to make things work."

Stan Cullis, the great Wolves manager who was Wright's first captain at the club, had much the same view – he always believed that Wright was destined to fail as a manager. "I knew Billy wouldn't make it as a manager," he told a reporter researching Wright's *This Is Your Life* TV appearance. "He was far too nice. You need a ruthless streak and the skin of a rhinoceros. Billy liked to be liked, but you just cannot be a football manager and also popular with everybody." If managerial

failure was the price to pay for his enduring popularity, you suspect Wright was ultimately comfortable with the bargain.

In 2019, Wright's daughter Victoria had an idea to create a digital memorial of her father's life. It was intended to be a present to her own daughter on her 25th birthday. Victoria had never seen her father play and her daughter had never known her grandad, taken away by cancer in 1994 at the age of just 70.

Having used her savings to create the film with the aid of many of Wright's former teammates and friends, Victoria reached out for extra funding from potential well-wishers. So overwhelming was the response from the public to her request that she contacted Wolves and the initial idea of a present became an evening in celebration of Wright. It is a great shame that her father didn't live long enough to see himself cast in bronze outside his spiritual home.

Billy Wright never won the World Cup. He never got to shake hands with the Queen as a proud and glorious England captain. He was only victorious in two of his ten matches at major international tournaments. But his legacy was secured in the manner of his approach and the consistency of his performance and affection in difficult circumstances.

Wright remains a beacon of English sporting history and integrity, his country's greatest-ever captain. His sporting life was a lesson in perseverance and the reward for dedicating yourself to treating others as you would have them treat you.

Opposite: Wright is held aloft by teammates Don Howe (right) and Ronnie Clayton (left) after England beat Scotland in April 1959. Wright earned his 100th cap in the match.

Left: Wright leads out England alongside Scotland captain George Young (left) ahead of England's fixture against Scotland at Wembley Stadium in 1957.

Above: Wright poses with a selection of his England caps. He would later give many away to well-wishers and children.

CHAPTER SIX

THE MARCH
TO GREATNESS

1960s

WALTER WINTERBOTTOM HAD REASON TO BELIEVE THAT THE WORLD CUP IN 1962 MIGHT BE DIFFERENT. THE TOURNAMENT TOOK PLACE IN SOUTH AMERICA AGAIN, BUT THE COOL CLIMES OF CHILE WOULD BE A SHARP CONTRAST TO THE STIFLING HEAT OF BRAZIL IN 1950. ENGLAND HAD ENJOYED TOTAL DOMINATION IN THE 1960–61 BRITISH HOME CHAMPIONSHIP, SCORING 19 GOALS IN THREE MATCHES THAT INCLUDED AN ASTONISHING 9–3 WIN OVER SCOTLAND AT WEMBLEY.

The modernisation of English football that Winterbottom had long craved was also finally arriving. Professional footballers had long enjoyed the status of local heroes, entertaining ordinary people as they cut loose from the tedium of daily working life, but they were hardly high earners. In 1960, the maximum weekly wage of a footballer in England was set at £20, and dropped to £17 in the summer. The salary gap to the average worker had narrowed over time.

In 1961, the Professional Footballers' Association took a stand. Led by Fulham inside-right Jimmy Hill, it called on its members to take strike action to campaign for the abolition of both the maximum wage and the "retain and transfer" system that gave clubs absolute power over their players. Stanley Matthews, once a vocal critic of

the abolition, offered the PFA his support. The players and their association were successful, first over wages and then the transfer system. England international Johnny Haynes became the country's first £100-a-week footballer.

Although the long-term effects of the shift would take time to trickle down, English football had a new future. Players' desire to reach the top of their game, and thus earn the kind of wages that would make them financially secure long after retiring, increased dramatically. So did the standard of the average footballer. Players took greater ownership of their fitness and preparation, keen to extend their time at the top. Younger players developed more quickly and clubs' scouting networks grew in a rush to discover them.

Winterbottom's confidence might have been dented by England's desperate showing in the 1961–62 British Home Championship, where England finished outside the top two (including ties) for the first time since 1937 and were winless in the competition for the first time in 34 years, but that was tempered by the suspicion that England had merely focused their attention elsewhere. In the build-up to Chile, England had beaten Austria, Spain, Italy and Mexico and brushed past Portugal and Luxembourg in World Cup qualifying.

The 1962 World Cup was, ultimately, another disappointment for England. Winterbottom's side were comfortably beaten by a Hungary team that had been ravaged by the effects of the Hungarian Revolution in 1956, and drew 0–0 with Bulgaria in a poor last group game (albeit with England knowing that a draw was enough for qualification to the knockout rounds). The 3–1 victory over Argentina was a high point, and England at least competed with Brazil for long periods of their quarter-final, but the squad returned home having completed their fourth World Cup without winning a knockout match.

At the beginning of August 1962, six weeks after the defeat to Brazil, Winterbottom publicly announced his resignation as England manager. If his 16-year tenure became defined by England's slump from self-professed inventors of the game to also-rans on the international stage, perhaps that said as much about the challenges of the job as his own performance. There was at least a recognition – within the game, the national media and the general public – that he

had done a great deal to change the game, both practically and behind the scenes. His successor led England to glory, building that great monument to English sporting success, but it was Winterbottom who laid the foundations.

Winterbottom's resignation caused – partly by design and partly by happy accident – an irrevocable shift in policy that would ultimately give birth to the modern England team. A six-man committee was formed to create a shortlist of managerial candidates, but their first two choices, Jimmy Adamson and Dennis Wilshaw, were met with public scepticism and ruled themselves out of the running.

The popular public choice was Alf Ramsey, the former Tottenham and England right-back who had taken Ipswich Town from the Third Division to the Championship title. Ramsey had achieved unlikely glory on a meagre budget by developing and improving players, instilling a wonderful team spirit, ruling his squad with a steely discipline and constructing an innovative tactical strategy that opponents struggled to cope with. On the surface at least, he appeared an ideal candidate for international management.

The only issue was Ramsey's insistence on having full control of team selection. In an interview with the *Daily Mail* in September

Opposite: Bobby Charlton attempts to dispossess Brazil's Garrincha during their 1962 World Cup quarter-final in Viña del Mar, Chile.

Above: Ray Wilson slides in on Garrincha during the World Cup quarter-final. Brazil would eventually win the tie 3–1.

 "I THINK ENGLAND WILL WIN THE WORLD CUP IN 1966. WE HAVE THE ABILITY, THE STRENGTH, CHARACTER AND, PERHAPS ABOVE ALL, PLAYERS WITH THE RIGHT TEMPERAMENT. SUCH THOUGHTS MUST BE PUT TO THE PUBLIC, AND THE PLAYERS, SO THAT CONFIDENCE CAN BE BUILT UP."

ALF RAMSEY, IN 1963, ON ENGLAND'S CHANCES OF WINNING THE 1966 WORLD CUP.

1962, he made his feelings clear: "England should appoint a manager on exactly the same basis as a club appoints a manager. He must be allowed to pick his team alone and to decide how players will play. I think an England manager must make up his mind what players he has and then find a rigid method for them to play to…"

The Football Association agreed to this shift in ethos and Ramsey was delighted to accept the offer on those terms. England now had a manager who was successful in club football, was at the height of his powers at the time of his appointment, and had a home World Cup to pour all of his energy into. Ramsey would also have three full years to design a strategy that would maximise home advantage.

Ramsey's first game in charge ended badly. Winterbottom had drawn the first leg of a European Nations Cup play-off round 1–1 with France, but Ramsey's team then lost 5–2 in Paris. But there were extenuating circumstances – the desperately hard winter of 1962 had delayed football's calendar to such an extent that the third round of the FA Cup suffered 261 postponements and was not completed until March. That defeat against France, coupled with hosting the World Cup, meant that England did not face a competitive fixture outside of the British Home Championship for more than three years.

Improvements came quickly as Ramsey built a core of players – all his own selections – that he believed could form the backbone of a World Cup squad. England drew 1–1 with Brazil at Wembley and beat Czechoslovakia, East Germany, Switzerland and a Rest of the World XI that formed part of the FA's centenary celebrations.

By August 1963, Ramsey – never short of confidence – was bullish about England's chances in 1966: "I think England will win the World Cup in 1966. We have the ability, the strength, character and, perhaps above all, players with the right temperament. Such thoughts must be put to the public, and the players, so that confidence can be built up."

Without the inaugural European Nations Cup in 1964 to participate in, Ramsey instead decided that England should take on a gruelling summer schedule that consisted of seven matches in five countries over 31 days that included fixtures against Uruguay, Brazil, Argentina and Portugal. Ramsey's theory was that – even if England suffered defeats in the humidity of Brazil – they would never again be surprised by an opponent in a major tournament. As luck would have it, England were then drawn to play three of the same opponents in the summer of 1966 and were unbeaten against all of them. Ramsey might have concluded that luck barely played a part – preparation is a blanket that can be placed over fortune.

Opposite: Ramsey talking to England players Bobby Smith (left), Jimmy Greaves (centre) and Maurice Norman (right).

Above: Ramsey watches on during a training drill at RAF Stanmore in February 1963.

Over the next 12 months, Ramsey formulated the mix of players he believed would be key to England's World Cup campaign. In a 1–0 win over Hungary (their first against that nation since 1936) at Wembley in May 1965, the first six names on England's team sheet – Banks, Cohen, Wilson, Stiles, Charlton J. and Moore – would be the same as those listed for the final against West Germany 15 months later.

In December 1965, when England won 2–0 against Spain in Madrid's Estadio Bernabéu, Ramsey recalled a young Alan Ball to great effect. England's eleven that night was missing only Martin Peters and Geoff Hurst from the actual World Cup Final team sheet. Those two would make quite the difference.

That Spanish victory was viewed as a key match in the build-up to England's eventual triumph. Walter Winterbottom's England had typically used a 4-2-4 formation that looked to exploit the majesty of Stanley Matthews and Tom Finney as wingers, but their time on the pitch had long passed. So too, Ramsey believed, had that formation.

England ostensibly lined up in a 4-4-2 formation, but each midfielder took a turn to push forward and create a 4-3-3 shape. Their constant movement and the variety of England's attacks – and the personnel within it – made it impossible for the Spanish to cope. By the time they had reacted to an alternative England midfielder advancing, the danger had been created. After the match, *The Sun* newspaper branded this new-look England as the "Wingless Wonders", and a new moniker was born.

Above: Jimmy Armfield (left) and Alfredo Di Stefano exchange pleasantries before England's match against the Rest of the World in 1963 that marked the FA's centenary celebrations.

Opposite, clockwise from top left: England's Bobby Smith is sandwiched while attempting to head the ball; Smith attempts a diving header; and Jimmy Greaves shoots past goalkeeper Milutin Šoškić to give England a 2–1 win.

Ramsey's formation maximised the talents of the midfielders who pushed on to support attacks, but it also demanded intense physical and tactical commitment. Those midfielders were also expected to track back and block any counter-attacks from their opponents. If opposition sides were able to break free, the great Bobby Moore was used in a sweeper role to extinguish any danger. There have been few better sights in the history of England's national team than Moore, captain by example, sliding in to steal the ball from an attacker's boot.

With their formation now set in stone, England enjoyed a busy run-up to the World Cup, at Ramsey's behest. Seven fixtures were scheduled between February and the opening match against Uruguay. They broadly fell into two categories – rough, tough contests against established nations (West Germany, Scotland and Yugoslavia) and gentler assignments against those who had not qualified for the tournament (Norway, Finland, Denmark and Poland). England won every one.

Ramsey's principles for the tournament were simple. He would take the squad to a training camp at Lilleshall that he had used a year earlier (clubs had been persuaded by the FA to be more willing to release players for international preparations) in a deliberate ploy to escape from big cities and the traditional footballing hotbeds of

England. Ramsey wished to prepare his squad in detail. Players slept in dormitories and were asked to submit to a relentless and regimented schedule of training, resting and team bonding with games of badminton, tennis and darts. Not every player may have enjoyed the monastic experience, but all were sensible enough to go along with it. They sensed something special building.

And how couldn't they? The national team, for so long dogged by less-than-ideal preparation and having to travel to far corners of the globe in search of glory, were seeing everything come together exactly as Ramsey had envisaged. They were prepared physically; they had experience playing against many of their forthcoming opponents; they had steeled themselves for the slog of tournament football when one mistake might decide the fate of a contest; they had forged a remarkable team spirit; they had a strong tactical plan; and they were in form.

The England team was ready. England was ready.

Below and opposite: Joe Baker (in white) scores England's opening goal against Spain in the Estadio Bernabeu in December 1965, and celebrates.

PROFILE:
SIR ALF RAMSEY

The most telling lines in Alf Ramsey's managerial career were not spoken during the break before extra time in the 1966 World Cup Final, when he urged his players on to victory, but roughly an hour later. With the England team jubilant in the dressing room, having been presented with their trophy by the Queen, Ramsey took Bobby Charlton to one side.

"What the bloody hell do you think you were doing out there?" was Ramsey's irritated question. "Shooting when you should have been looking around for other people. We should have had it sewn up." The pursuit of perfection is relentless for those whose personalities demand it. Crowning glory is merely a step along the road.

Ramsey was a man out of place even in his own time. The sixties in England were a decade in which the country moved – literally and culturally – from black and white to technicolour, into a world full of freedom and ambition. Ramsey was part of the old school, his military history giving him a schoolmasterly air that belied his middle age.

The stories of Ramsey's disciplinarian tendencies are legendary. John Smith, a trainee player at Ipswich Town, was told that he could no longer wear winkle-picker shoes because they were "not becoming of a professional footballer". When Bobbys Charlton and Moore arrived back shortly after curfew before an away tour, Ramsey arranged for their passports to be laid on their pillows, ensuring a sleepless night. In the morning, the manager explained that if it had been practical, he would have left them both behind.

But it's not true to suggest that Ramsey ruled with an iron fist. Like all great managers, he calculated the right times for tight discipline and friendly leniency. Despite high competition for places that inevitably led to several players feeling ignored, none had a bad word to say about the manager.

Ramsey had earned his chance to be England's first dedicated full-time manager and there's little doubt that the strength of his CV persuaded the FA to let him have full control over team selection. He had joined an Ipswich Town that was down on its luck, in the third tier and without any obvious ingredients for rapid transformation.

Within six years Ramsey had Ipswich in the First Division, where they won the league title during their first-ever top-flight campaign. It remains one of the most astonishing periods in the history of any English club. In November 1962, they beat AC Milan 2–1 at Portman Road but were eliminated from the European Cup. By then, Ramsey had already been confirmed as Walter Winterbottom's successor.

Opposite: Alf Ramsey watches from the bench as England beat Romania in the 1970 World Cup.

Above top: Ramsey embracing England's players as they hold the World Cup after beating West Germany in the final in 1966.

Above: Ramsey leading England training. Bobby Moore (left, in white shirt) stands behind him.

Above, clockwise from top left: Then-Tottenham player Alf Ramsey practises his heading; Ramsey standing on the terraces at Ipswich Town's Portman Road ground for the last time before taking the England job; and Ipswich Town, managed by Ramsey, celebrate their league title victory in 1962.

Left: Ramsey and his coaching staff watch on as the 1966 World Cup Final unfolds.

Opposite: Ramsey supervising an England training session in 1969.

The headline for Ramsey's England story was written in the summer of '66, but his greatest achievement was to create the bold tactical plan that would make the win possible. He quickly identified that the traditional use of wingers needed to be abandoned due to England's lack of options in the position and, in doing so, forged a team and a style that was able to hold its own physically, dig in defensively and yet display the star attacking qualities that could turn tight matches. If his football was criticised for its lack of style, that often spoke more about other teams' attempts to combat England; because when play opened up, Charlton, Peters, and Hurst or Greaves, would punish the opposition. Just as groundbreaking – and ultimately difference-making – was his approach to match preparation and acclimatisation. We cannot know if England would have won the World Cup without their pan-American tour of 1965, but the desire to scout opponents – three of whom they then played at Wembley – was invaluable.

England's World Cup success should not create a false image of Ramsey avoiding scrutiny before the tournament. Few in the media truly bought into the manager's insistence that England could win the tournament, and several were suspicious that he had failed to justify his control over team selection. In their lower moments, the press labelled the team "Ramsey's Robots" and there were clearly a few journalists waiting with pens at the ready if England had faltered. Eventually, Ramsey took away their ammunition.

Ramsey's England never again hit the heights of that World Cup. If their performance in the heat of Mexico in 1970 made their quarter-final exit easier to stomach (and England were deeply unfortunate to be drawn against perhaps the greatest international team in history

in the group stages), their poor showing in the 1972 European Championship (ending in a 3–1 aggregate quarter-final defeat to West Germany) and failure to qualify for the 1974 World Cup (just three goals in four matches) gave some credence to the theory that Ramsey was a lucky manager rather than a good one.

But that seems deeply unfair, not least because of what came before and after him. England have had more talented squads than his, enjoyed more favourable tournament draws than he did and never again matched his achievements. Perhaps that criticism speaks of Ramsey's uneasy relationship with the media. In his later years, he admitted some regret over his lack of openness with the press.

But then that was Ramsey, a private man who only ever wanted what was best for his team and his country and never once reneged on those principles despite being handed multiple chances to do so. He shunned the limelight, shunned praise and shunned financial opportunity – it was estimated that Ramsey turned down £280,000 in commercial opportunities during his tenure. He believed that only by setting the perfect example to his players could he demand perfection from them.

If that integrity stopped Ramsey from guaranteeing the financial well-being that his service surely merited, you suspect that he would never have wished it any other way. If England underperformed post-1966, that became the exception rather than the rule long after he departed. Ramsey was simply a man and a manager who vowed to do his best, safe in the knowledge that nobody could ask for anything more. During one glorious year, his best was enough to place him among the immortals of English football.

CHAPTER SEVEN

THE 1966 WORLD CUP

JACK CHARLTON FELL TO HIS KNEES, UNABLE TO PROCESS WHAT HE HAD ACHIEVED WITHOUT MOMENTARILY STAYING STILL AND ALLOWING HIMSELF A FEW SECONDS OF PRIVATE REFLECTION. BOBBY SHED A TEAR AS HE WALKED TO EMBRACE HIS BROTHER. RAY WILSON HIT HIS HANDS ON THE TURF, AS IF CALLING THE COUNTRY TO CELEBRATION ON A GIANT DRUM. NOBBY STILES AND GEORGE COHEN HELD EACH OTHER BEFORE STILES DANCED HIS FAMOUS JIG.

Around them, their teammates reacted to the magnitude of a national triumph achieved by a precious, glorious few. Only Sir Alf Ramsey remained resolute, standing on the touchline and refusing to share the players' limelight. This was their legacy, being played out in real time as if part of a glorious dream sequence. Ramsey had promised that England could win it and even, in his more bullish moments, insisted that they would. He had justified that bullishness in the most spectacular fashion.

In the stands, supporters chanted Ramsey's name and thronged together. Some waved Union Jack flags or wore Union Jack hats, others were adorned with rosettes to mark the occasion of the final. A few stuffed toys of World Cup Willie, the official mascot, were lifted above the heads of supporters and danced above raised hands as if bobbing along in an ocean.

Across the country, people spilled out into the streets in celebration of the long wait for glory. The most fervent celebrations were undoubtedly in London, where hundreds gathered in Trafalgar Square and an exhilarated few danced in its fountains. A giant conga formed, singing and twisting as it gallivanted across the concrete.

Sometimes only time and hindsight can define the true greatness of a moment. At Wembley Stadium on July 30, 1966, everyone present was acutely aware that they had witnessed something historic. England, who for so long had stuttered and stumbled in its attempts to reinforce its position as not just the inventor of modern football but also an excellent exponent of it, had finally stepped up to the challenges of the expectation, the pressure and the occasion.

Right, above: The crowd celebrates during an England match at Wembley Stadium in the 1966 World Cup.

Right: Bobby Moore embraces Nobby Stiles after England's 2–1 semi-final win over Portugal.

Opposite: Jack Charlton sinks to his knees as the final whistle blows in the World Cup Final, unable to comprehend the magnitude of their achievement.

If the England team ended July 1966 as the toast of the nation, they began it amid an air of national cynicism and doubt. Bobby Moore's West Ham contract had expired on June 30, and without club affiliation he was technically ineligible for the England team, before a temporary deal was struck. There was still significant doubt among journalists about England's ability to compete with the best in the world. And in a distinctly soap-opera storyline, the World Cup trophy itself had been stolen and was eventually found by a dog – Pickles – and its owner.

England's first games hardly put any lingering doubts about the team's quality to rest. Their opening 0–0 draw was against a Uruguay side that put 10 men behind the ball. England were forced to resort to long-range shots and could barely muster a clear-cut opportunity. If Uruguay's defensive approach was a backhanded compliment to England, the Wembley crowd didn't see it that way. Full time was met with virtual silence broken only by the sound of whistles as the players left the field. It was the first time that England had failed to score at Wembley in 52 post-war matches.

England improved against France and Mexico in their second and third group games, defensively solid but hardly entertaining in two regulation 2–0 victories. Following the win over France, Ramsey reproached his players for the only time during the tournament: "England were not up to the standards of their two previous performances. Far too much casualness spread into their play. They were a little irresponsible."

Elsewhere in the country, things were slowly falling into place for England. North Korea had caused the biggest World Cup shock since England's own defeat to the United States by beating Italy 1–0 at Middlesbrough's Ayresome Park; Italy were eliminated after the group stage.

So too were much-fancied Brazil, unbeaten at the World Cup for 12 years before their defeats to Hungary and Portugal, both of whom progressed. The Brazilians – with good reason – cried foul about the rough treatment administered to Pelé, which went unpunished. Pelé initially declared that he would never play in another World Cup.

England were acutely aware that Argentina had enough individual talent and shared grit to trouble them, and they were arguably the team most similar to Ramsey's left in the tournament. But if Juan Carlos Lorenzo's side had earned a reputation in the group stage for excessive physicality and provocative behaviour, they doubled down on it at Wembley in the quarter-final.

Antonio Rattin, Argentina's captain and personification of the team's style – for better and for worse – became the game's defining player. He had already been booked by referee Rudolf Kreitlein but continued to protest every decision and question the official's authority. When Luis Artime was being booked for a bad tackle, Rattin spoke out of turn one too many times and was sent off.

Chaos ensued. Rattin initially refused to leave the field and was backed up by his teammates in a demonstrative display of mutiny towards Kreitlein. When Rattin did eventually depart – with his teammates not following through their threat to follow him – England had their chance. Martin Peters created a yard of space with 13 minutes remaining and his West Ham teammate Geoff Hurst headed home the winner.

If Argentina had tried to unnerve England with brawn, Portugal believed brains were the best strategy. They had overcome a significant scare against North Korea in their quarter-final but were saved by the brilliance of Eusebio, arguably the greatest player in the world at the time.

The semi-final was the antithesis of England's previous match. Portugal were determined to play a fluent, technical attacking game that England's defence were at their magnificent best to thwart – Stiles was supreme in his close handling of Eusebio.

Above: Jimmy Greaves in action against Uruguay in England's first group game of the 1966 World Cup.

Opposite, clockwise from top left: Referee Rudolf Kreitlein is escorted from the pitch under police protection after sending off Argentina's Antonio Rattín against England; Geoff Hurst celebrates scoring his winning goal against Argentina (top and bottom right); Ramsey does his best to stop George Cohen (right) swapping shirts after the game; Kreitlein is knocked off his feet after an accidental collision with Argentina's Oscar Más.

> "IT'S GOING TO BE THE BIGGEST DAY OF YOUR LIVES AND YOU ARE GOING TO WIN. GOODNIGHT, GENTLEMEN."
>
> ALF RAMSEY

The Portuguese did not commit a single foul until the 57th minute, but were eventually undone by the magnificence of Bobby Charlton's efficiency. He scored after half an hour to relieve the pressure on England, and extended that lead with 12 minutes remaining with a fabulous finish.

Even a late Eusebio penalty – awarded after a Jack Charlton handball – was not enough to wrest control from England's self-anointed destiny. Portugal had torn into England towards the end of both halves and could consider themselves unfortunate to have lost an exceptional contest. But Stiles, Charlton and England had persisted and resisted any fear of collapse. They had faced dour, defensive teams, teams that tried to physically intimidate them, and a team with impeccable technical ability. Only West Germany were left to conquer.

As England's players went through their pre-match superstitions and made their way to Wembley, a mood of celebration had already engulfed the stadium, with vast swathes of supporters confident of victory. Every inch of the place was packed with those lucky enough to have secured a ticket; thousands who had begun the tournament doubtful and reticent about extolling nationalistic self-regard were ending it closer to their national team – literally and figuratively – than they could have dreamt. German flags occasionally pockmarked a sea of red, blue and white and a mass of journalists, photographers, cameras and officials filled the England dressing room.

Ramsey shook the hand of each player and avoided a grandstanding, motivational team talk. England's manager had delivered his simple message the evening before: "It's going to be the biggest day of your lives and you are going to win. Goodnight, gentlemen."

West Germany started the final in the ascendancy and soon established an advantage. Ray Wilson made a rare mistake, allowing Helmut Haller to score from inside the box. But England roared back almost immediately, as if desperate to dissipate any fears among each other and the crowd. Moore's free-kick was met by the head of Geoff Hurst, afforded an unforgivable amount of space, and England were level.

England were marginally in control of a final that ebbed towards its conclusion with the scores still level, until Alan Ball won a corner and took it himself. The set piece was thwarted but the ball was never cleared. Martin Peters benefited from the spin on the ball and volleyed past Hans Tilkowski.

Opposite, from top: West Germany defender Wolfgang Weber equalises to take the World Cup Final into extra time (top left); Geoff Hurst scores England's third goal with the referee agreeing the ball had crossed the line (top right); and Martin Peters scores England's second goal in the final (bottom).

Below: Hurst's hat-trick goal, capturing him for eternity in mid-air with the ball about to hit the net and seal triumph for England.

And then came the twist that might have destroyed a legacy. With West Germany's final attack of normal time, they were given a questionable free-kick. With the ball drilled into the penalty area more in desperate hope than expectation, a scramble led to defender Wolfgang Weber sliding to direct the ball past Gordon Banks's dive. There were claims for a handball but referee Gottfried Dienst was unmoved.

If ever there was a time for a manager to make a difference, *the* difference, this was it. England were surely half-broken by the late equaliser and West Germany must have considered themselves holders of a psychological advantage. But Ramsey was resolute: "You've won it once. Now you'll have to go out there and win it again," he told his players. "You think you're tired? Look at them."

And so it proved. The controversy surrounding Hurst's second goal and England's third persists to this day, to the extent that it has become its own myth: the more anyone purports to provide a definitive answer, the more disagreement it will provoke and the further it takes us from that definitive answer. The only conclusion that mattered to Ramsey and England was that the goal was awarded then.

It was a truly remarkable conclusion. Hurst's final shot, which provoked the iconic "They think it's all over…" commentary from Kenneth Wolstenholme, was the 62nd of the match – 31 apiece. It was England's 11th shot on target, one more than West Germany. But that final goal added a layer of gloss to England's victory and removed some of the immediate focus on the goal-line controversy.

What is also remarkable in hindsight is Hurst's reaction after his third goal. A man who was unsure of his place on the eve of the game, who had just become the first hat-trick scorer in a World Cup Final, and who had confirmed his nation's victory in a home World Cup, simply jogs across the penalty area, almost apologetically accepting Alan Ball's wild embrace. Perhaps this was simply fatigue. Or perhaps Hurst was caught momentarily unaware of, or drowned by, the magnitude of what he – and his team – had just achieved. Hurst later admitted that, even by the early hours of the next morning, it hadn't struck him that he had done anything out of the ordinary.

England's post-match celebrations were reflective of the time – ceremonial and comparatively understated. They began with a government reception from which the team proceeded to an FA banquet at the Royal Garden Hotel on Kensington High Street, where thousands of fans gathered to salute their new sporting heroes.

Between courses, the players spilled out onto the balcony to receive their due adoration. Ramsey, typically, was unenthusiastic about being the centre of attention. But the chants of the crowd in his favour did persuade him to offer a cheery wave and a gesture of his gratitude.

The true joy lay not in the celebrations but in the sheer magnitude of the achievement. The cheers were merely a sideshow, an immediate outpouring of joy over something that would provide a lifetime of cherished anecdotes and infinitely more memories. As Bobby Charlton would later say: "As soon as the final whistle went I said to my brother, 'You know, Jack, life for us will never be the same again.' And I was right."

Right: English football's most iconic photo, captain Bobby Moore carried aloft by his England teammates with the Jules Rimet Trophy raised in his right hand.

PROFILE:
BOBBY MOORE

If English football is caught in a moment, Bobby Moore is literally central to that image. The afternoon of July 30, 1966, at shortly before 6.00pm, England's captain was held aloft by his teammates, sitting on the shoulders of a nation. A few minutes earlier, Moore famously wiped his muddy hand on the tablecloth before shaking hands with the Queen. He was the perfect sporting hero for England's perfect sporting triumph.

Moore was not just England's captain, but their natural leader. Three years earlier he had become the youngest-ever player to wear the armband, and by the time the World Cup came around he had established himself as a fine central defender, having converted from a wing-half. Along with West Ham teammates Martin Peters and Geoff Hurst, Moore would parade the Jules Rimet Trophy at away grounds around England.

It therefore seems unthinkable that Moore could have been absent from that day. On the eve of the tournament, with England's captain seeking a move away from West Ham, his club refused to budge. Had Moore stayed firm he could have been left without a contract and ineligible for the final, but national team manager Sir Alf Ramsey intervened.

Then, three days before the final, Moore was struck down with tonsillitis, mercifully diagnosed early by a team doctor. "Dr Alan Bass got cracking right away but if we had left matters for a day, the tonsillitis would have got such a hold on Bobby it would have taken five days to clear up," coach Harold Shepherdson remembered. "That is how close Bobby was to missing the final."

"My captain, my leader, my right-hand man," said Ramsey of his captain. "He was the spirit and the heartbeat of the team. A cool, calculating footballer I could trust with my life. He was the supreme professional, the best I ever worked with."

Many more agreed with Ramsey. When the world team of the 20th century was selected in 1998, Moore was selected at centre-back alongside Franz Beckenbauer, the only player from the British Isles to be picked. And Beckenbauer was under no illusions as to the pecking order of that team's defenders. "Bobby Moore was the best defender in the history of the game," he said.

Most famously, Moore was an incredibly modern defender. In an age when a "cultured" centre-half might be the one who said "good morning" before he scraped his studs down the back of your ankle, Moore was not a physical player. Nor did he pride himself on aerial ability, another staple of that position.

He was not even particularly quick. Instead, he relied on anticipation, a reading of the game that would become the backbone of future defensive greats. As Scotland manager Jock Stein once famously remarked: "There should be a law against him. He knows what's happening 20 minutes before everyone else."

"If speed is only a matter of taking yourself physically from A to B, then I'm not fast," Moore said. "But isn't it important to know earlier than the next man that it's necessary to go from A to B? Isn't speed of thought as vital as how fast you can move your legs? I like to think I compensate for my slowness by seeing situations quickly, by anticipating and reacting before others realise what is happening." He became the master of that art.

If English football peaked in 1966, Moore did so four years later in Mexico. Amid accusations that he was past his best at the age of 29,

Opposite: Moore leads England on to the pitch ahead of the World Cup quarter-final against Argentina.

Above: Moore kissing the Jules Rimet Trophy as England lap the pitch following the final in 1966.

Right: Bobby Moore leads out England before their 1–0 victory over Scotland at Wembley in May 1973.

his performance in defeat against Brazil is one of the greatest by an England player. His tackle on Jairzinho, who scored in every one of Brazil's matches, is regarded as one of the best in the game's history. Moore waits and tracks, waits and tracks, then dives in to take the ball off the winger's toes.

As the game ended in a Brazilian victory, Moore did not collapse in frustration or anger, but embraced Pelé in a sporting gesture that is still considered one of football's most iconic moments. The greatest-ever player against his toughest opponent, in Pelé's own words.

More so than 1966, this was Moore's moment. He was a champion, of course, but more so a competitor and a gentleman. He would come second in the Ballon d'Or that year, behind Gerd Müller.

Unfortunately, Moore's retirement was not always a happy one. Having been overlooked for coaching roles by the FA, he received the same treatment from West Ham, with whom he had argued after they repeatedly refused his requests to let him leave. Moore had numerous failed business ventures, including losing a large percentage of his career earnings in a collapsed investment scheme.

It was these setbacks that ex-wife Tina blamed partly for the break-up of their marriage. "I could see that the man was being torn apart," she said. "He was wondering what the hell was going on. Self-doubt started to creep in. Mentally it was a very dreadful thing." The worst was still to come.

Moore had first battled cancer in 1963, the year he was made England captain. He had an operation to remove a cancerous testicle, and returned to professional football after an astonishingly brief period of three months. That illness was only revealed after his death, Moore preferring to keep it secret in order to avoid stigma.

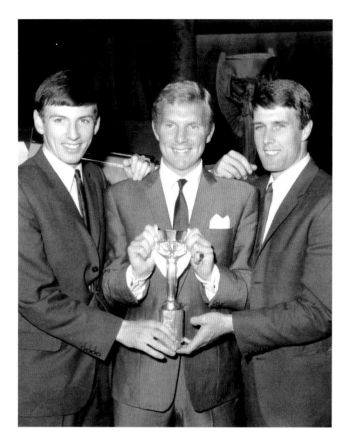

By April 1991, Moore had another operation, this time to remove a tumour from his colon. On February 14, 1993, he publicly announced that he was suffering from bowel and liver cancer, which had spread. Three days later, he commentated on England v San Marino, now a frail man ravaged by devastating illness. Seven days after that final public appearance, Moore passed away.

Moore's death, coming so soon after his revelation of serious ill health, shocked the nation. The first member of England's World Cup-winning team (or staff) to pass away, the personification of our national team's success, had been taken away at the age of 51. A symbol of that glorious summer had been lost.

"Immaculate footballer. Imperial defender. Immortal hero of 1966. First Englishman to raise the World Cup aloft. Favourite son of London's East End. Finest legend of West Ham United. National Treasure. Master of Wembley. Lord of the game. Captain extraordinary. Gentleman of all time," reads the inscription on the pedestal of his statue outside Wembley. Every word of it is true. Every word of it will remain so for as long as that statue stands.

Opposite, from top: Moore collects the Jules Rimet Trophy from Her Majesty the Queen (top); and is photographed as he arrives in Mexico ahead of the 1970 World Cup (bottom).

Above: Moore poses with the Jules Rimet Trophy, flanked by final goalscorers Martin Peters (left) and Geoff Hurst (right).

Right: Moore and Pelé embrace after their titanic tussle at the 1970 World Cup. The image would come to embody fair play and sportsmanship.

PROFILE:
SIR BOBBY CHARLTON

Football could so easily have lost Bobby Charlton, and would have been infinitely poorer as a result. When Manchester United's plane crashed on the runway at Munich-Riem Airport on February 6, 1958, Charlton was badly injured but luckily was sitting in a spot from which goalkeeper Harry Gregg could pull him from the wreckage. Even then, the easy thing to have done would have been to retire from the game. Charlton had lost eight of his teammates and carried with him the psychological burden of survival.

Instead, he chose the opposite path. That terrible night propelled him to play for the memory of those lost in Munich and its aftermath, and to help rebuild Manchester United in their honour. Perhaps "chose" is a misnomer; this was more about duty. On that night, and in Munich's Rechts der Isar hospital, Charlton, without knowing it, began a journey that would transform him from young fledgling to the rock around which a new team would be built.

Still, we must not underestimate the strength of character and mental resolve required to cope with that burden. Without it, every loss can feel as if you're letting down those whom you lost and every victory can feel incomplete without them. And you can obsess so much over the performances of the team that you forget to take care of your own well-being. But Charlton dealt with it all impeccably. He runs like a seam through Manchester United's history, a talisman to those who were robbed of the chance to play their part in it.

Ranking Charlton among the pantheon of the great English footballers surely misses the point. There is no benefit, and no obvious logical process, to ordering players from different eras. But one thing is certainly true: no English player in history has enjoyed such a remarkable purple patch as Charlton. Between 1965 and 1968, he won two league titles and the European Cup with Manchester United, the World Cup with England, and was named as the Ballon d'Or winner (1966), or runner-up, three years in succession.

This was the stuff of comic book heroes. In the space of almost exactly a decade, he had suffered career-threatening injuries, lost friends and colleagues, recovered from physical and mental trauma, stepped up when his club needed him most and underpinned the greatest sporting triumph in his country's history.

Opposite: Bobby Charlton taking a moment to prepare himself ahead of England's game against Germany in the 1970 World Cup. It would be his final international appearance.

Above: Charlton scores his second goal as Manchester United beat Benfica 4–1 to win the 1968 European Cup.

Below: Charlton holds the Jules Rimet Trophy above his head, alongside Alan Ball (left) and Bobby Moore (right).

That disaster shaped Charlton's life, but it did not define it. "Sometimes I feel it quite lightly, a mere brush stroke across an otherwise happy mood," he wrote in his autobiography. "Sometimes it engulfs me with terrible regret and sadness – and guilt." The only way to shake off that unwarranted guilt was to make people proud of him on and off the pitch. Charlton never once fell short.

It is Charlton's consistency for England that creates his legacy, the record scorer for his country until Wayne Rooney eclipsed him in 2015. His 106 caps came across 12 years, and Charlton remains the only England player to be named in four different World Cup squads. His peak came in the semi-final in 1966, when he wrested control from Portugal with a goal in each half and overshadowed the great Eusebio, whom he pipped to the Ballon d'Or that year by a single vote.

Charlton prided himself on the versatility that made him a manager's dream – he played at right-half, inside-right and as a deeply-lying forward for England, and was continually able to drop into space to pick up possession. Sir Alf Ramsey demanded that his attacking players worked back in his wingless system and there were few players he cherished more than Bobby.

"Early in my management, I knew I had to find a role suitable to Bobby's unique talents," Ramsey later recalled. "He wasn't just a great goalscorer, with a blistering shot using either foot. Bobby was a player who could also do his share of hard work." On multiple occasions, Ramsey referred to Charlton as the linchpin of his World Cup-winning team.

But it would be remiss not to focus on his individual assets: a shot – particularly from distance – so powerful that Denis Law would run straight at goalkeepers who were liable to spill the ball as a result, a speed that belied his frame and an unerring ability to predict the best space to drop into to cause the most panic.

And yet what stands out most to those who knew and played with and against him was not Charlton's shooting, his ambidexterity or his teamwork; it wasn't anything that could be proven in the red of Manchester United or the white of England. It was his kindness and his humility.

Sir Matt Busby described him as the most popular footballer he had ever worked with: "As near perfection as a player and man as it is possible to be." Sir Alex Ferguson, Bobby's great friend whom Charlton mentored during his Manchester United management, agreed: "The great attribute of Bobby – and it's a great example to anybody who has been successful – is how he has kept his feet on the ground and retained his humility all his life."

It is those personality traits that made him the everyman hero. George Best had the pizzazz and the unattainable natural talent, but Bobby was a different breed. He was the boy from Ashington who simply adored football, and who overcame unspeakable tragedy to sit on top of the world but never once gloated in his achievement.

Opposite, from top: Charlton scores his – and England's – second goal against Portugal in the 1966 World Cup semi-final (top); and the Charlton brothers return to the North East after helping England win the World Cup (bottom).

Above: Charlton holds aloft the European Cup after his goals helped Manchester United to win the trophy for the first time.

Right: Charlton leaves the field after England's World Cup exit to West Germany in 1970, with Alf Ramsey looking on.

CHAPTER EIGHT

THE FALLOW YEARS

1970s

IT'S NOT EASY BEING THE BEST TEAM IN THE WORLD. HAVING SPENT YEARS TARGETING OUTSTANDING TEAMS SUCH AS BRAZIL, WEST GERMANY, ITALY, ARGENTINA AND OTHERS IN A BID TO PROVE THAT THEY WERE WORTHY OF SUCH COMPANY, ENGLAND SUDDENLY FOUND THEMSELVES THE NATURAL TARGET FOR OTHERS – AND NEVER MORE SO THAN DURING THEIR 3–2 BRITISH HOME CHAMPIONSHIP DEFEAT TO SCOTLAND AT WEMBLEY IN 1967. TRAINFULS OF SCOTTISH SUPPORTERS SANG AND DANCED THEIR WAY BACK HOME, PROCLAIMING THEMSELVES THE NEW WORLD CHAMPIONS. JUST NINE MONTHS AFTER THEIR GREATEST DAY, ENGLAND SUPPORTERS AT WEMBLEY FELL SILENT.

Sir Alf Ramsey was not worried by any post-World Cup comedown, even after England had failed to win the European Championship in 1968, for which they started as favourites. Yugoslavia were the eventual victors after a physical, gruelling quarter-final that had included England's first-ever red card (shown to Alan Mullery with minutes remaining). But they recovered to beat the Soviet Union in the third-place play-off and had qualified ahead of their home nation peers, atoning for the Scotland defeat. All focus now was on defending their World Cup success.

Ramsey firmly believed in England's chances in Mexico and that was not mere bluster. With the rise to prominence of English clubs in European Continental competitions (Manchester City and Manchester United both won cups between 1968 and 1970), the development of Alan Ball, Colin Bell, Peter Osgood, Francis Lee and Martin Peters, and experienced players from 1966 still dotted throughout the squad, Ramsey considered his pool of players to be better than four years earlier.

England's manager had also done his homework again. With England automatic qualifiers for the tournament, Ramsey arranged a tour of South America in the summer of 1969 that saw England face Brazil, Uruguay and Mexico. They were unfortunate to lose to Brazil after taking the lead.

But if England's form had improved since the European Championship – that loss to Brazil was their only defeat between the two tournaments – there were growing concerns about the style of their football. Between July 1968 and May 1970, England scored only 28 times in 17 matches; 18 of those came in just five games against France, Belgium, Northern Ireland and Scotland. Some in the media believed Ramsey was retreating too far into a defensive shell.

The 1970 World Cup was not easy for England. Matches were played in stifling heat and humidity, the team hotel was subjected to incessant night-time noise from locals keen to gain any advantage, and they were forced to train and play at altitude. Bobby Moore was the subject of accusations of theft that England firmly believed were a set-up and they were handed the worst possible group-stage draw; Brazil were the pre-tournament favourites.

Having comfortably beaten Romania – albeit by only one goal that came midway through the second half – England prepared to face the mighty Seleção in a lunchtime kick-off in which the temperature nudged 100 degrees Fahrenheit. They started brightly, controlling the game until Jairzinho's cross was met by the stooping head of Pelé. Brazil's striker was already celebrating as Gordon Banks somehow dived low to his right and clawed the ball up and over his crossbar. It became the most famous save in the history of the game.

The longer the game continued, the more Brazil controlled possession in the heat and the more England understandably tired. The winning goal came on the hour, Pelé holding off England defenders for long enough to create space for Jairzinho, who powered the ball past Banks.

Having made five changes for a must-not-lose final group game against Czechoslovakia, which England won 1–0 thanks to an Allan

Opposite: Three action shots of Gordon Banks'
'Save of the Century' from Pelé at the 1970 World Cup.

Clarke penalty, England faced a West Germany team desperate for revenge in the quarter-finals. Again, preparation was not smooth. Mexico barred England from flying to Leon, forcing them to take an uncomfortable 170-mile coach journey to a motel on the outskirts of town that was shared with the families of the West Germany squad. On the eve of the game, Banks was afflicted by a stomach bug (that he later suspected was a deliberate plot) and Ramsey was forced to call upon Chelsea's Peter Bonetti.

Perhaps it is that game more than any other that came to define England's toils over the subsequent decades. Had England held on to their commanding 2–0 lead in the Guanajuato Stadium, they would have considered themselves favourites to beat an Italy team that had won only once in the group stage and against whom England had never lost in an official international. Even defeat in the final to Brazil

in a South America-based tournament would have allowed England to retain the lustre earned in 1966.

But England did conspire to lose. Ramsey was criticised for his substitutions, choosing to rest Bobby Charlton for the semi-final and replacing Martin Peters rather than the injured Keith Newton. Bonetti was certainly at fault for West Germany's first goal, allowing Franz Beckenbauer's shot to squirm under him; Banks would surely have saved it. After West Germany equalised, forcing extra time, it was England who looked psychologically and physically defeated. Gerd Müller, that great goalscorer, issued the final, bitter blow with 11 minutes of the 120 remaining. It would be 12 years before England played another World Cup match.

In hindsight, perhaps that would have been the right time for Ramsey to move on to a technical position from which he could organise coaching

and preparation on a national basis. But his England team had hardly disgraced themselves in Mexico, and the sharp knives of Fleet Street were easy to ignore when England won their first five games following the World Cup; the 93,000 who came to Wembley in November 1970 hardly seemed perturbed that Ramsey was still in the dugout.

Even so, England were fading. They qualified for the Euro 1972 play-offs (effectively a two-legged quarter-final) but were again beaten by West Germany, this time outclassed at Wembley by a side moving in the opposite direction. In attempting to qualify for the 1974 World Cup, England finished behind a Poland team that were rank outsiders when the campaign began. Needing a victory in their final group game against the Poles at Wembley, England had 26 corners, twice hit the woodwork and forced a string of saves from Jan Tomaszewski, but only drew 1–1. Their era of ascendancy was over.

So too was Ramsey's tenure. Accused of inflexibility by a media that had long been suspicious of his continued suitability for the job, and with the public less enamoured with his wingless football when the goals – and results – dried up, the Football Association realised that a change was necessary. On May 1, 1974, Ramsey was formally sacked, though the decision had been made the month before.

Former Aston Villa and Manchester City manager Joe Mercer was appointed on a caretaker basis, and lost only one of his seven matches in charge, but there was only ever one likely permanent candidate once Don Revie had phoned the FA to make his appetite for the position clear.

Like Ramsey, Revie had proved his capabilities in English club football, taking Leeds United to two First Division titles, three other domestic trophies and two Inter-Cities Fairs Cups, having been appointed when Leeds were still in the second tier. But Revie was also a controversial figure, accused of using rough tactics in pursuit of victory and methods that some felt would not be easily transposed on to the international game. But nobody could doubt his charisma or his record. After an exploratory meeting in which Revie proved he understood the demands of the role, he was named as England's third permanent manager. It was viewed – in the media and among the public – as a coup by the FA to attract the best manager in the country.

Revie's era started with great promise. England beat Czechoslovakia 3–0 in his first match in charge, which was also the first Euro 1976 qualifying game. Five months later, England welcomed West Germany to Wembley in the hope of laying down a marker of their future intent.

Opposite above: West Germany's Gerd Müller scores the winning goal past Peter Bonetti during England's World Cup quarter-final defeat in 1970.

Opposite below: Bobby Charlton leaves the field after defeat to West Germany (left); and West Germany's players celebrate Uwe Seeler's equaliser that took the game into extra time.

Below: Martin Peters is crestfallen as Poland celebrate qualifying for the 1974 World Cup at England's expense.

The Germans were missing Gerd Müller, Paul Breitner, Uli Hoeness and Günter Netzer, but this was still an experienced team and they were formidable opponents. Revie's England, with seven changes made from their previous game and caps given to three debutants, controlled the midfield and won 2–0.

But behind the scenes, issues were stacking up. Several senior players reportedly disliked Revie's team-building exercises, believing the manager attached too much importance to them and too little importance to on-pitch form.

More frustration came with Revie's penchant for making regular changes to the team, often giving England an air of transience that had hallmarks of the selection committee era. Four or five changes to the starting eleven became commonplace, with certain players expressing reservations that they were never sure of their place. If it was Revie's intention to motivate players to perform at their best in each game he was mistaken.

Either way, that West Germany win was the high point for Revie's England. England lost the return fixture against Czechoslovakia in Bratislava and failed to beat Portugal both in Lisbon and at Wembley. Worse was to come in the British Home Championship: England lost to Scotland in 1976 (finishing second), and to Scotland and Wales in 1977 to finish third.

With the relationship between the England manager and his employers becoming strained, Revie needed a successful qualification campaign for the 1978 World Cup. That was made infinitely more difficult by England's lack of seeding. They were handed the nightmare draw of Italy in a four-team group from which only one country would progress.

Again, Revie was undone by his tinkering to the team. England travelled to Rome unsure of the starting eleven, but Revie opted to start both Stan Bowles and Brian Greenhoff and made six changes from the victory over Finland just five weeks earlier. The defence had never played together, while seven of the Italy team played for the same Serie A club, Juventus. The result was a comprehensive 2–0 defeat that effectively consigned England to also-rans in the group.

Three months later, in England's next match, they suffered the same margin of defeat and a similar dismantling at the hands of a fantastically entertaining Dutch side containing Johan Neeskens and Johan Cruyff. The media reaction was predictable and brutally honest. *The Times'* Norman Fox compared it to the first Hungary defeat in 1953: "If anything, this latest embarrassment was even more revealing than the first opening of our eyes… it highlighted the inadequacies for all to see."

Revie's eventual departure was laced with intrigue and mystery. In June 1977, England again flew out to South America for a three-game tour of the continent in preparation for the following summer's World Cup, a tournament it now seemed unlikely that England would participate in. But England were managed by Les Cocker for their opening game of the tour, against Brazil. Revie flew off to watch Finland v Italy in preparation for the vital qualifier against Italy in November.

In fact, while Revie did indeed watch the Finland game, he then flew to Dubai to hold secret talks with the Football Association of the United Arab Emirates (UAE) over the possibility of becoming their national coach, with a remit to expand the game in the region. The UAE FA had first approached Revie in March 1977, but were knocked back. This visit was an indication of interest.

Upon his eventual arrival in South America, Revie attempted to abdicate his position as manager, claiming that he believed his work had become impossible due to nebulous factors outside of his control. That offer was rejected, and Revie stayed in place.

Later came the news that rocked the FA. On July 12, 1977, with a sealed envelope containing details of the story still unopened at

Below: Giancarlo Antognoni of Italy celebrates scoring the opening goal during the World Cup qualifying match in Rome in November 1976. Italy would win the game 2–0.

Opposite: Don Revie is pictured taking an England training session in February 1977.

Above: Don Revie with Trevor Cherry during a friendly between England and Argentina in June 1977. Cherry would later be sent off.

Below: Joe Mercer (right) walks with Trevor Brooking (left) at an England training session in Belgrade, during Mercer's period as caretaker manager.

Opposite: Ron Greenwood taking an England training session. Greenwood succeeded Don Revie in 1977.

 "IF ANYTHING, THIS LATEST EMBARRASSMENT WAS EVEN MORE
REVEALING THAN THE FIRST OPENING OF OUR EYES…
IT HIGHLIGHTED THE INADEQUACIES FOR ALL TO SEE."

THE TIMES' NORMAN FOX COMPARING THE LOSS TO THE DUTCH WITH THE HUNGARY DEFEAT OF 1953.

FA headquarters, Revie's employers learned of his resignation to take up the position in the UAE via a story in the *Daily Mail*. An FA commission initially banned Revie from involvement in English football for 10 years, although he returned to the High Court in 1979 and had the ban revoked.

With England now in some disarray on the pitch and with the FA facing an off-field crisis following Revie's messy departure, a firm hand on the tiller was desperately required. Success was only possible when players, managers and officials were all on the same page.

Ron Greenwood became the standout candidate. He was out of work at the time which, on the eve of a new season, avoided the need for the FA to negotiate the release of employed coaches from their contracts. He was an innovative manager who believed that style was a vital ingredient of winning, and that Corinthian spirit was popular within the FA. He had achieved great success at West Ham with a number of players who formed the backbone of England's 1966 triumph. And he was seen as diplomatic and unlikely to cause a repeat of the controversy that had hampered the national team under Revie.

In fact, the strongest negative argument was not that Greenwood was unfit for his appointment, but that he should have replaced Ramsey in 1974, when he was still West Ham's manager, and before he had moved upstairs to become the club's general manager. Nevertheless, the FA had their man. Greenwood initially acted as caretaker for three matches in 1977, and then held the job permanently for another four and a half years.

In the context of their disappointments and ultimate underperformance, it's tempting to frame the 1970s as a wasted decade for the England national team. They played only four major tournament matches in the decade, all within its first seven months, and won only twice. At a time when English clubs were beginning to dominate European football, with four consecutive European Cup winners between 1977 and 1980, the England national team never quite found the harmony that Liverpool and Nottingham Forest nurtured under iconic club managers.

But football works in never-ending cycles. If failure can hang around the necks of a team and a governing body, another opportunity to display resolve and earn redemption lies just around the corner. The time for bickering and tinkering was over. England needed a stalwart to take them back to where they believed they belonged, and in Greenwood the FA believed that they had found one. Now it was time to earn back their place among the world's elite.

Opposite: England's Steve Coppell skips away from Italy's Claudio Gentile during their World Cup qualification match at Wembley in November 1977.

Above: England's Trevor Brooking is chased by Marco Tardelli during England 2–0 win over Italy.

PROFILE:
THE TRAILBLAZERS

As Viv Anderson walked out of the Wembley tunnel on November 29, 1978 and on to the pathway that led to the turf, the noise engulfed him. Ninety-two thousand supporters were not there to see him – Anderson was not arrogant enough to believe that – but they were present to witness history. After 106 years of England senior matches, Anderson would be the first black player to pull on the shirt.

nderson had a mixture of emotions at his first call-up. He had earned his place, a 22-year-old right-back who was blossoming under the stewardship of Brian Clough and who had won his first league title six months earlier. He was incredibly proud of the honour and legacy that his first international cap guaranteed.

But Anderson was also keen to point out that he was simply doing his job to the best of his ability, and that he owed so much to those who had come before him and those who were enduring the same fight for equality. He had grown up watching Clyde Best at West Ham and namechecked Cyrille Regis and Laurie Cunningham.

Cunningham was the first black player to win a cap for England's Under-21s. Cyrille Regis was a beacon for those who came after him, a wonderful ambassador for black excellence. Over the next six years, Mark Chamberlain, Luther Blissett, Ricky Hill, John Barnes, Brian Stein and Danny Thomas would all play for England.

And although Anderson's debut was a seminal milestone in the history of the England national team, it would be wrong to say that it signified a moment of enlightenment in the attitude towards black players and the abuse they received.

English football witnessed overt and hateful racist abuse aimed at black players and black supporters. They had to suffer a torrent of monkey noises, had bananas thrown at them, were spat at, and were routinely verbally abused by more than just a small minority in the crowds. It would be worse at away grounds, but even home supporters would hatefully express their displeasure at having black players in their team. Former player Chris Kamara detailed the hate he received from Portsmouth supporters during his time at the club in the mid-1970s, who then had a strong National Front representation in their home crowd.

It is hard to comprehend just how difficult it must have been to perform in such circumstances. Regis spoke at length about how it fuelled

Opposite: Viv Anderson walks on to the Wembley pitch ahead of his England debut in 1978. Anderson was the first black player to win a cap for England's senior team.

Above: Ben Odeje, who became England's first black representative at any level when he played for England schoolboys at Wembley in March 1971.

Below: Anderson watches on as Steve Coppell dribbles with the ball against Czechoslovakia. Anderson was making his debut in the match.

"NO DOUBT THERE ARE PLAYERS WHO HAD THE POTENTIAL BUT DID NOT MAKE IT BECAUSE OF THE ABUSE THEY SUFFERED."

MARK SUDBURY, AN FA OFFICIAL OVERSEEING THE ANTI-RACISM CAMPAIGN.

his desire to be at his best, turning the abuse against those who aimed to use it as an advantage. That is to Regis' great credit, but others may not have managed such strength of character. How many careers were broken, how many lives altered forever, by what they were subjected to?

In 2001, the FA issued an official apology for that abuse. Starting in the 1990s, they embarked on a wide-scale initiative platformed by chief executive David Davies, FA board member David Dein, and Gordon Taylor, the Professional Footballers' Association's chief executive. But they also felt it important to accept that more could and should have been done to protect players in the 1970s and '80s, believing that such an admission was crucial in embracing a new commitment to help tackle the problem. Mark Sudbury, one of the FA officials who oversaw the anti-racism drive, was at pains to make

a dispiriting point: "No doubt there are players who had the potential but did not make it because of the abuse they suffered."

One way to silence the racists was to normalise the presence of black players and celebrate those who used their excellence as a powerful tool. Ron Greenwood gave debuts to Anderson, Regis and Cunningham between 1978 and 1982, and vowed to always pick players on merit with no regard for their skin colour. Sir Bobby Robson gave caps to

Opposite: Cyrille Regis wearing his England Under-21 shirt. Regis became a high-profile anti-racism campaigner.

Below: Luther Blissett celebrating at the end of England's 9–0 European Championship qualifying win over Luxembourg in 1982. Blissett had just scored a hat-trick.

nine different black players between 1982 and 1984, including Barnes in 1983. Barnes was probably England's most naturally talented attacking player for a half-decade period in the 1980s, and there's no doubt that his excellence – including the mesmeric goal in the Maracanã in 1983 – did much to quieten many of the doubters.

Much progress has been made since then. We must celebrate that the current England squad has such a high black representation and, more than that, we must celebrate that nobody ever gives it a single thought. When Ollie Watkins scored on his debut against San Marino in March 2021, nobody stopped to think that he was the 102nd BAME player to win a senior England cap. He was just Ollie Watkins, of Aston Villa and of England.

And we must pay homage to those who enabled that normalisation. To Anderson, and his first cap. To Regis and Cunningham, and their wonderful skill and determination to ignore the abuse. To Luther Blissett, the first black scorer of an England hat-trick. To Barnes and his supreme talent. To Paul Ince, who became the first black captain of England against the United States in 1993. To Hope Powell, England's first black head coach at senior level.

But amidst those celebrations, we must also recognise that there is still much work to be done – this fight never stops and the moment we believe we have won we begin losing. Fans can rightly point to the lack of representation from players of Asian heritage as an example of how the national team isn't yet truly reflective of our nation. The rise of social media and a growing extremism among some supporters, too, has led to a cavalcade of incidents in which black footballers have received abhorrent abuse; one incident is too many.

England's highest-profile black players have taken it upon themselves to lead the fight. They are prepared to work with social media companies, anti-racism groups and the game's stakeholders to make life better for those who follow them, just as Anderson, Regis, Blissett and many others did before them.

This commitment to positive change represents the best of England and the best of the England team. It is an environment in which the most talented and the most dedicated individuals in their profession can aim to achieve greatness together whatever their background and whatever their skin colour. The fight to preserve that opportunity is, unfortunately, a never-ending one. But it is forever worth pursuing.

Above: Hope Powell playing for England against Scotland in 1997. She would become the manager of the England women's team the following year.

Opposite: Marcus Rashford sprints for the ball against Belgium in England's UEFA Nations League group match in October 2020.

CHAPTER NINE

THE RE-RISE OF
THE WOMEN'S GAME

1880s – 1970s

ALTHOUGH THE ENGLAND WOMEN'S TEAM ONLY PLAYED THEIR FIRST INTERNATIONAL MATCH IN 1972, IT WOULD BE DEEPLY REMISS NOT TO REFLECT UPON THE GREATER HISTORY OF THE GAME IN THIS COUNTRY AND ON THE NOW-OUTDATED ATTITUDES THAT DELIBERATELY LIMITED ITS PROGRESS. THIS IS A STORY OF STRUGGLE THROUGH ADVERSITY, THE RIGHTEOUS FIGHT FOR OVERDUE RECOGNITION AND DETERMINED PERSEVERANCE.

On May 7, 1881, just nine years after the England men's team played in their debut international against Scotland, Edinburgh's Easter Road hosted a match between two teams from either side of the border. The Scottish team was led by Helen Graham Matthews, an activist for women's rights who believed that football should not be an exclusively male pastime. The England captain is not recorded, and many of the team were thought to use pseudonyms to hide their identity from those who believed women should not play football. A report in the *Glasgow Herald* noted a crowd of over a thousand spectators was present.

Nine days later, the two teams met again in Glasgow when the match was interrupted by a male-dominated 500-strong crowd, some of whom invaded the pitch and jostled several players. Injuries were only avoided because of a police presence that drove the supporters from the pitch, but media reports were – perhaps unsurprisingly – unsympathetic. "'Ladies' football has had an exceedingly short life, and not a very merry one," wrote the *Leeds Mercury*. "Public feeling has demonstrated against the unseemly exhibition."

But that prediction proved to be entirely inaccurate. During the first two decades of the 20th century, the participation and interest in women's football grew exponentially. The outbreak of the Great War, and the necessary mass employment of women in munitions factories to assist with the war effort, gave men and women a chance to play football together on their breaks. The most famous club in the history of the women's game – Dick, Kerr Ladies FC – was born out of exactly that scenario.

Dick, Kerr Ladies were remarkably successful. In 1920, they played a series of four international exhibition matches against France and later toured the country, playing games in Paris, Le Havre, Roubaix and Rouen. That inevitably created a significant amount of public interest in England (the England men's team, for instance, did not play the French until 1923) and, on Boxing Day in 1920, the Dick, Kerr Ladies' fixture against St Helens Ladies at Goodison Park attracted a crowd of 53,000, with

thousands more turned away because the stands were full. The average crowd in the men's First Division that season was just below 18,500.

But within a year, women's football had been banned by the FA. Whether that was because of concern at the crowds and public interest in the women's game at a time when the FA were committed to expanding the men's game, or a worry about the public image of women as successful sportspeople during an age when society viewed women as subservient to men (women couldn't even vote until 1928) is open to debate, but the official explanation was dubious: "…the game of football is quite unsuitable for females and ought not to be encouraged."

But women's football did carry on – matches, training and participation did not cease overnight. In 1922, The English Ladies' Football Association held their cup and 23 different teams entered a competition won by Stoke Ladies, who beat Doncaster and Bentley Ladies in the final. Women's football's epicentre in England remained in the North West, where Preston Ladies (formerly Dick, Kerr Ladies), Blackpool Ladies and St Helen's Ladies were among the strongest teams in the country; Hey's Brewery Ladies of Bradford were arguably the best team in Yorkshire.

But female players were deliberately ostracised from the framework of the national sport. They were no longer permitted to play on FA pitches, any organised national league was impossible, the dream of an era of full-time players was destroyed, teams were often forced to train on scrubland and in municipal parks, and of the few players who could earn recognition for their skills, many opted to move abroad to countries where they could be financially rewarded for their talent.

Opposite above: The Dick, Kerr Ladies team pose for a photograph during their historic 1922 tour of North America.

Opposite below: Artist's drawing of Dick, Kerr Ladies playing against Hey's Ladies at the Burnley Cricket Club ground.

Left: A Dick, Kerr Ladies team photo, taken in 1921.

And so the knock-on effect of the ban became devastating. The Lyons Ladies and Huddersfield Atalanta, two high-profile women's teams of the age, shut down. The ELFA did not file any accounts between 1922 and 1931, when it was formally dissolved. By the 1940s, the number of women's clubs had dwindled sufficiently to make a league structure impossible, with clubs forced to resort to playing exhibition matches or raising funds for foreign tours. Women's football culture was never destroyed, but it was operating with a firm foot placed upon its head.

England's World Cup success in 1966 predictably caused a huge upsurge in interest in football and spurred a boon in the grassroots game, which included women. With more women wanting to play the game, small clubs began to form that – to mirror the 1910s – were often affiliated to businesses and workplaces. Their number grew rapidly until local leagues began to form.

By 1969, attitudes were changing within the FA. In November of that year, members of 44 women's clubs met to form the Women's Football Association (WFA), and by 1971 the FA had rescinded its ban on women playing on its pitches. That year, the WFA held its first knockout cup competition, then named the Mitre Trophy. It would ultimately become the Women's FA Cup.

With UEFA and FIFA slow to catch on, a group of Italian businessmen created the Federation of Independent European Female Football (FIEFF), which hosted international tournaments in 1970 and 1971. Harry Batt, secretary of the Chiltern Valley women's team, organised a squad of English players to compete in tournaments that travelled to Italy in 1970, finishing fourth, and Mexico in 1971, where they lost group games to Mexico and Argentina. Batt's squad attended the opening ceremony in Mexico City's Azteca Stadium in front of a crowd of 100,000 spectators.

In 1972, with the women's game now fully recognised by the FA, former Queens Park Rangers and Watford forward Eric Worthington was asked by the WFA to arrange a squad to play Scotland in the first official international match for England, which would take place at the Ravenscraig Stadium in Greenock on November 18, 1972, almost 100 years to the day after the first men's international between the same countries.

The match was the brainchild of Pat Gregory and Elsie Cook, the secretaries of the English and Scottish WFAs respectively. Gregory later recalled that there was no deliberate motivation to make history or become trailblazing pioneers for women's sport in both countries: "We were having an international match, which seemed the logical thing to do. We were just playing a game. There were no grand thoughts." But the impact was grand, all the same.

It was a cold and inauspicious day, not reflective of its significant place in our sporting culture. The Scottish team had no financial backing and bought kits from Glasgow Rangers using a loan. Cook bought badges and numbers and stitched them onto the shirts herself.

But the encounter was fiercely contested and surprisingly close given that the WFA had a pool of 200 players to pick from and Scotland had

Opposite: The England women's team in a changing room at Wembley
Stadium, training ahead of their first official fixture in November 1972.

Above top: England goalkeeper Sue Buckett before England's first official
fixture against Scotland in 1972.

Above: The England women's team pose for an official photo before the game.

just six teams at the time. England won 3–2, but had trailed 2–0 after goals from Mary Carr and Rose Reilly, before Sylvia Gore, Lynda Hale and Jeannie Allott saw England roar back. With heavy snow falling and substitutes forced to watch the match from underneath thick blankets, England held on. Their ban was over. Their new era had begun.

With Eric Worthington moving to Australia for a role as the director of coaching at the Australian Soccer Federation, the WFA appointed John Adams for England's next two matches. Adams was a regional coach for the FA and was later honest enough to admit that he had little enthusiasm for the task ahead of a two-day training camp in Matlock, before the team left for an international in France.

But Adams was enthralled by both the quality of England's players and their appetite for learning through coaching, something the men's game – with its more rigid attitudes and traditions – often struggled

to take on board. Adams had consulted with Sir Alf Ramsey on a strategy for training and decided to work on team play, and defending and attacking set pieces.

Adams' planning worked beautifully. England beat France 3–0 and Scotland 8–0, with eight of their 11 goals coming from set pieces. He left his position as planned, but with his preconceptions of the women's game turned on their head.

Adams' full-time replacement was Tommy Tranter, who had played amateur football and gained the highest coaching qualification within the FA's system to become an FA Full Staff Coach. Like Adams, Tranter was initially uneasy about taking the job because of his reservations about the organisational structure of the women's game, and the time he would be afforded with amateur players.

But Tranter became one of the great allies of the women's game. He lobbied for a more professional set-up and arranged extended training camps to work with the squads. He introduced discipline

"YOU'D TRAVEL WHEREVER YOU WERE TRAVELLING ON A FRIDAY, YOU'D TRAIN ON SATURDAY AND YOU'D PLAY ON SUNDAY. AND AS YOU CAN IMAGINE, THAT'S QUITE DIFFICULT WHEN YOU'RE WORKING FULL-TIME AND PLAYING WITH A TEAM THAT YOU DON'T REALLY KNOW."

ENGLAND INTERNATIONAL ELAINE BADCOCK

and training that would not have looked out of place in the men's professional game at the time. He researched how best to get girls involved in football at a young age, and concluded that those with older brothers often had a head start.

But more importantly, he treated his players as footballers. He saw no skill gap between male and female footballers, merely a system that had been weighted against the latter for too long. He saw no reason to alter training to fit women's sport, but instead trusted them to match his demands. And he defended them against a media that was, at the time, laced with ingrained sexism. As one sneering journalist wrote: "It is hard to resist the temptation to snigger a bit at women playing soccer. But don't do it in front of Tommy Tranter."

Unsurprisingly, England flourished under Tranter's stewardship. Between 1973 and 1976, his team lost only to Sweden and Italy, two countries that had an established culture of women's club football far beyond England's. Particular highlights were a 2–0 victory over France at Plough Lane in November 1974, two wins against the Netherlands in 1974 and 1976 and a 1–0 win over Italy at the same ground, which was viewed as a huge coup.

———

For all the on-pitch improvements during Tranter's tenure, life as an international women's footballer was not easy in the 1970s. At every turn they were met with discriminatory attitudes from men who demeaned their abilities and questioned the relevance of the women's game. More often than not, they were forced to juggle full-time jobs with their sporting commitments and would play exhibition matches of five-a-side games to stay fit between training camps.

Elaine Badcock was called up for the national team in 1976. In an interview with *inews* in 2019, she recalled working shifts at the AirBus factory in Chester where she would be allowed to leave early when she was training with England.

"You'd travel wherever you were travelling on a Friday, you'd train on Saturday and you'd play on Sunday," Badcock said. "And as you can imagine, that's quite difficult when you're working full-time and playing with a team that you don't really know." She remembers playing two charity matches in Italy and having to ask their opponents to wash their kit for the second fixture.

Sandra Choat played for England between 1974 and 1977 and recalls the logistical hurdles her club team had to clear just to play regular matches. "Amersham's manager, Joe Debenham, had a fruit and veg van," Choat told *WFA History*. "On a Saturday evening he would clear out all the produce and most of the waste (but not the smells) and convert it with benches into our football coach for our

long away trips. We would pile in our kit bags and ourselves, chugging up the motorway at 40mph, billowing out thick smoke."

Their memories are a few of many shared by every member of those nascent squads. If the culture of women's football in England had proved that it had survived the 50-year ban and England's early results suggested promise for the future, the next task was to implement an organisational structure to oversee the growth of the sport and formalise the relationship between the England team and the grassroots game. With Trantor stepping down from his position in 1979 and moving to coach in Iceland, the Women's Football Association aimed to appoint a replacement who could lead the team into a new age.

Opposite: Members of the England women's team training at Wembley in November 1972. In the centre is Sylvia Gore, who scored their first ever official goal.

Above: Eric Worthington, appointed as the first ever manager of the England women's team in 1972.

PROFILE:
SHEILA PARKER

Sheila Parker grew up with football. She played games in the park and in the street from the age of eight, the only girl in a sea of young boys in the 1950s with dreams of turning professional. And she was better than them too, delighting in knocking the ball one side of an opponent and running around the other. Parker wore shinpads, just in case any boy got a little miffed by the treatment. At weekends, she would stand and watch Chorley FC, her local team in Lancashire, aiming to pick up tips on teamwork, communication and technique that she could hone and practise during the week.

That in itself made Parker different. She remembers her mother being confused at having a daughter who was so into football at a time when gender stereotypes were still so entrenched in British society, and getting changed behind the stair door to try and hide her mud-covered clothes after games in the rain.

If societal norms and organisational roadblocks promised to make a life in football incredibly difficult for Parker, she did have one advantage. Being raised in Chorley placed her near the closest thing that existed to a hub of organised women's football in England. At 13, Parker joined Dick, Kerr Ladies. She would eventually go on to play for Chorley Ladies, St Helens, Preston and Fodens, a works team from Sandbach that shocked Southampton to win what was then known as the WFA Cup Final in 1974. Parker never had to leave the North West.

But the life of a successful women's footballer was hardly a dream. Parker remembers playing on farmers' fields, getting changed in outhouses, seasons pockmarked by gaps without matches, and hastily arranged games in different parts of the country due to the lack of a league structure. Parker had grown up outperforming the boys but with no hope of a full-time career or even semi-professionalism.

But the formation of the Women's Football Association (WFA) in 1969 did prompt a change in Parker's career and her life. After Eric Worthington had been asked to host trials and choose a squad for the first fixture against Scotland in Greenock in 1972, Parker was picked not just to start the game but to captain England.

As with her teammates, Parker did not approach the fixture with the overt sense that the players were creating history, but she did later recall an overwhelming rush of pride that came immediately after the match. Parker was 24 years old, had only recently returned to football after the birth of a child (something that at the time often caused women to retire from playing), had continued to juggle amateur pursuit with professional career and had become the de facto leader in a new era of women's football in England.

Parker won 33 caps for England at a time when fixtures were at a premium. She was an incredibly versatile footballer: central defence for most of her England career, central midfield when required. Then as a striker for Preston, she scored an astonishing 51 goals in 14 matches to win them the league in 1975. Parker's only regret was that she was not able to turn professional; she would surely have been widely recognised as a star if that had been possible.

Opposite: Sheila Parker posing for her official England photo on the pitch at Wembley.

Below: Parker training with teammates at Wembley in 1972.

Parker later recalled that her fondest memories as a player were the early away trips with England: France, the Netherlands, Switzerland and Sweden. But this wasn't just a team broadening its horizons after years of fighting for recognition, nor was it just a group of women who became great friends through the significance of their collective experiences. This was a group of footballers who had always loved playing the game and who appreciated the opportunities that were denied to women born even 10 years earlier.

That created an extraordinary camaraderie within the camp that manager Tommy Tranter was able to utilise. It was not enough to go out and enjoy playing the game, even if that is a vital ingredient of success. Those early England players understood that they had a responsibility to commit as much as they could to their improvement and development because they were role models for the next generation of girls who could now feasibly grow up dreaming of playing for England.

Life was not easy for that team or for Parker. Funds had to be raised for trips and she worked full-time as a telephonist alongside her club football, fitness training and international career. When she retired from playing there were no obvious routes to staying in the game, so she trained and qualified as a referee in Lancashire instead.

Parker was inducted into the National Football Museum's Hall of Fame in 2013. She chose to donate an England shirt, scarf and her first three caps to the museum, understanding that if one young girl saw them on display and became inspired to push harder to become a footballer, her work would be done.

There is no exact lineage. Lucy Bronze, Rachel Yankey, Karen Carney or Kelly Smith did not become footballers because of Sheila Parker and her teammates. But that nascent England team, earning its reputation with landmark victories in the 1970s, did change the landscape of women's football in England. Their determination to push for recognition and their commitment to improvement after that recognition had been granted allowed those who followed them to have better facilities, greater funding and a footballing life that was just a little easier.

Below: Parker standing in front of her teammates as they prepare for an official team photo. Parker would captain the side in their first official match.

Opposite: Parker taking a break from England training at Isleworth's Borough Road College in September 1975.

CHAPTER TEN

SO NEAR AND
YET SO FAR

1980–1990

THE 1980s BEGAN WITH ENGLISH CLUB FOOTBALL FIRMLY AT THE TOP OF THE EUROPEAN GAME.

BETWEEN 1977 AND 1982, THE EUROPEAN CUP WAS PASSED AROUND BETWEEN LIVERPOOL,

NOTTINGHAM FOREST AND ASTON VILLA WHILE IPSWICH TOWN WON THE UEFA CUP IN 1981.

KEVIN KEEGAN WAS NAMED AS EUROPE'S BEST PLAYER IN 1978 AND 1979; THE ONLY OTHER

PLAYER TO WIN CONSECUTIVE BALLON D'ORS BEFORE HIM WAS THE GREAT JOHAN CRUYFF.

Ron Greenwood's England temporarily basked in the glow of that dominance. He had been unable to turn around a hopeless position in 1978 World Cup qualifying, but his England side embarked on a run of one defeat in 22 matches with Keegan as the attacking focal point of the side. They breezed through qualifying for Euro 80, dropping one point in eight matches, before winning high-profile friendlies in Spain, and against Argentina at Wembley.

Hopes grew that England had finally re-established themselves as a major tournament contender, boosted by a group-stage draw that saw them avoid 1974 World Cup winners West Germany, 1976 European Championship holders Czechoslovakia, and 1978 World Cup finalists the Netherlands.

Ultimately, England disappointed in Italy. Hampered by previous failures that ensured that virtually every member of the squad was making their bow at a major international tournament, England took the lead against Belgium in their opening game but that was the only high point. The game was marred by violence in the stands that caused Italian police to use tear gas which temporarily blinded Ray Clemence and caused a five-minute delay, but by then Jan Ceulemans had already equalised for Belgium. Defeat to Italy made qualification for the final impossible; even a victory over Spain became worthless with Belgium and Italy drawing their final fixture.

And thus began a period of gloom for Greenwood and England. A 2–1 defeat in Romania in October 1980 put England on the back foot in World Cup qualifying, exacerbated by a miserable run in the first half of 1981 that saw England secure only two 0–0 draws from six matches that included defeats to Spain, Brazil, Scotland and Switzerland.

At that point, Greenwood came close to resignation. On the flight back from Hungary on June 6, 1981 – a qualifier that England had won 3–1 to end their winless streak – the manager told captain Keegan of his intention to leave his position. It was only an intervention from several senior players, who crowded around Greenwood's seat on the plane, that persuaded him to stay. An away defeat in Norway three months later, soundtracked by the famous TV commentary of an ecstatic Bjørge Lillelien, did little to help Greenwood's mood.

But England were handed an unlikely reprieve. With Romania needing only one win from a double-header against Switzerland to consign England to ignominy, they lost in Bucharest and could only draw 0–0 in Berne. A home win against group winners Hungary and England would reach the World Cup for the first time in 12 years. Paul Mariner's goal, England's first at Wembley in five matches, caused jubilation in a packed stadium. Somehow, some way, England were going to Spain for the 1982 World Cup.

Even so, Greenwood had experienced enough to know that his time had come to an end. Buoyed by the achievement of qualification, he announced that the World Cup would mark the end of his tenure in charge. For all the success of English clubs in European competition, he expressed his dismay at the lack of domestic talent being developed. Many of the star players at those clubs – Graeme Souness, Kenny Dalglish, Alan Hansen, Arnold Mühren, Frans Thijssen, John Robertson, Ian Rush, Archie Gemmill, John McGovern – were not English. "Blame me for not producing the players of the quality required," Greenwood had said in defence of Sir Alf Ramsey when he left England. Here, he believed, was the proof.

Greenwood obviously needed a successor. Brian Clough was never considered a likely option due to his inflammatory, pointed opinions of the FA. Bob Paisley had turned 63 and was considered too close to retirement. That left Sir Bobby Robson, who had followed in Ramsey's

Opposite: Bobby Robson smiling before his first press conference as England manager in Copenhagen in September 1982.

footsteps at Ipswich Town and established them among the most successful clubs in the country. In 13 years at Ipswich, Robson had won the FA Cup, UEFA Cup, finished runner-up in the First Division in both 1981 and 1982 and arguably outperformed Ramsey, given the might of Liverpool, Nottingham Forest and Aston Villa at the time. Robson was offered the job before the World Cup and accepted it midway through the tournament.

The 1980s can be broadly defined as England's "what if?" decade. Include Italia 90 and England reached three World Cup finals and left each with a quiet sense of pride on the one hand, but a piercing regret at how things might have played out differently on the other. They would surely have traded reaching the final eight of each competition (and final four in 1990) for one seismic victory and a first major tournament triumph away from home soil.

In Spain, England ultimately paid for their early high performance. Bryan Robson scored 27 seconds into the first group game against France, and a 3–1 victory was followed by wins over Czechoslovakia and Kuwait during which England did not concede a goal. Thus, England progressed to the four-group second round, where they were the better team in a 0–0 draw against West Germany and unfortunate again not to beat Spain, although with only one of three teams from the group advancing to the semi-finals, they had required a two-goal margin of victory to qualify. England headed home having conceded one goal and never trailed at any point during the tournament.

They had reason to feel hard done by. While the second group stage brought a daunting draw for England with hosts Spain and West Germany, France, who had finished second to England in the first round, faced decidedly less intimidating matches against Northern Ireland and Austria in their second stage. There is little to be gained from preoccupation with ifs, buts and maybes, but England would have been clear favourites to win that group and reach the semi-finals.

But 1982 also marked the end of an era for England, and not just because Robson immediately took over the position of manager. Keegan and Trevor Brooking, whose injuries were – in Greenwood's view – the major factor in England not winning the World Cup, never played for their country again. Neither had started the crucial final match against Spain, much to their annoyance, especially as the game had shifted in England's favour following their introduction.

No England manager ever enjoys a long honeymoon period, but for Sir Bobby Robson the pressure upon his position – and thus his reputation – began almost immediately. The near miss of the 1982 World Cup created a national mood of expectation that he initially failed to satisfy, despite Greenwood's parting insistence that the job was an almost impossible one to perform successfully.

Robson's task was made more difficult by a necessary changing of the guard. Ten of England's 22-man 1982 World Cup squad were aged 30 or over; four of them were 33. Robson insisted that it was his responsibility to make a five-year plan for England that hinted at a preference for younger players, but that clashed with the relative paucity of emerging talent. Robson bestowed 14 new caps in his first 12 months alone, but of those 14, only John Barnes remained a fixture in the team throughout his tenure.

But Barnes himself was a leader of an important movement. Viv Anderson had become the first black player to win a senior cap for England in 1978, followed by Laurie Cunningham and Cyrille Regis in 1979 and 1982 respectively, and Robson continued that mark of progress. At a time when black players were routinely abused at football matches, Robson's second squad contained six black players. That was not always popular: a small group of fans sang racist songs on the flight home from Brazil in 1984. But Robson remained determined not to let the hateful minority win.

In Robson's first game, England drew 2–2 with Denmark, then lost 2–1 to West Germany in a friendly at Wembley. If those initial doubts were eased by comfortable away wins over Greece and Luxembourg, qualifying for Euro 84 became a slog that would ultimately defeat England. Robson unsurprisingly bore the brunt of the criticism. Between February 1983 and September 1984, England only once won two matches in succession. More instructive were the home defeats to Denmark and the USSR, the latter provoking protests by tabloid newspapers that insisted that the manager should quit.

But something changed in England from that night on. Whether Robson merely considered that he had nothing to lose, or whether – as Robson later intimated – the victimisation of the squad's black players created a spirit to fight adversity and unfair treatment, England reacted well to missing out on the European Championship. Instead, they

"BLAME ME FOR NOT PRODUCING THE PLAYERS OF THE QUALITY REQUIRED."

RON GREENWOOD

Opposite: Ray Wilkins attempts a shot against Denmark in a European Championship qualifier played at Wembley Stadium in September 1983 (top), while Allan Simonsen and Klaus Berggreen of Denmark celebrate during their 1–0 victory over England (bottom).

Left: Robson conducts a press conference in September 1982. He had been appointed two months previously.

embarked on a tour of South America and beat Brazil in the Maracanã, Barnes' goal one of the best and most famous in England's history. It helped, too, that Robson rejected Barcelona's overtures and that England were given a comparatively gentle qualifying group for Mexico 86.

A deeper pool of players emerged, too, thanks to the re-emergence of Everton as a force to challenge for domestic honours. While Liverpool's team contained a large number of Scottish, Irish and Welsh players, Everton under Howard Kendall relied upon a nucleus of English players who joined the England set-up en masse: Peter Reid, Trevor Steven, Gary Stevens and Gary Lineker, who signed in the summer of 1985. Their great goalkeeper was Welsh, but then Robson had Peter Shilton, who challenged Neville Southall to be considered the best in the country.

Perhaps the 1986 World Cup sums up England's experiences in the competition's long history better than any other. There was hope, triumph and ultimate despair, huge controversy, disappointing performances and dominant victories, a striker forging an international reputation, injury concerns over a star player and a team that both delighted and exasperated its public while leaving it desperate for revenge. And there was a quarter-final exit, comfortably England's most regular hurdle.

Left and below: The magician – Diego Maradona dances his way past another England player (top) before slotting the ball past Peter Shilton (bottom) during England's 1986 World Cup quarter-final.

Opposite: The thief – Maradona handles the ball past Shilton, unspotted by the referee despite England's protestations, to give Argentina the lead.

Only seven players from the 1982 squad went to Mexico, and that included Bryan Robson, whose injury had the nation, and the national team manager, praying for rapid recovery. England had not lost for 12 months and had a younger, fresher squad than in recent tournaments. Terry Butcher was the emphatically eldest statesman at 36, but no other player had yet reached 30. The squad had acclimatised to both the heat and altitude they would face in Mexico.

It did not begin well, with England beaten by Portugal after failing to take their chances and being punished for a defensive error that would leave Robson angry. They stood on the verge of early elimination after Bryan Robson walked off with a shoulder injury against Morocco and Ray Wilkins was controversially sent off. A 0–0 draw provoked catcalls and jeers from England's support.

But, as if to epitomise Robson's reign, England then improved. Lineker scored a hat-trick against Poland in the final group game as the manager made changes that achieved the desired response. Paraguay were beaten by the same 3–0 scoreline in the last 16 to set up a quarter-final against Argentina that would produce two goals that England supporters would never forget, however much they wished amnesia upon themselves.

England were left rightly aggrieved that Diego Maradona had the temerity to handle the ball so blatantly and that referee Ali Bennaceur, and his assistant, both failed to spot it. Maradona's second, game-clinching goal was a piece of majestic brilliance, but in Mexico City we saw two sides of Diego and England were punished by both. Robson was furious on the touchline: "I immediately knew it was a handball and I waited for the officials to sort it out."

England did receive criticism for their failure to attack Argentina sufficiently when the scores were level, as if somehow they had earned their own misfortune, but the clear focus remained on Maradona. Perhaps that helped England, although they hardly felt as much at the time. That quarter-final propelled them on four years later, desperate to atone for such injustice. It established a mood of sympathy around the squad that might not have been present if both goals were perfunctory. Ultimately, England missed out on a semi-final against Belgium that would have offered a wonderful shot at a second World Cup Final.

If Mexico earned Robson considerable goodwill and greater patience from the country's public and media, however, he came perilously close to exhausting it in the months that followed. England went to Euro 88 with problems – Butcher's broken leg, Lineker's illness, John Barnes and Peter Beardsley clearly fatigued, and Chris Waddle recovering from injury – but they became the first and only England team to lose every match they played at a major tournament. By the time England had drawn against Sweden and Saudi Arabia in late 1988, Robson's position appeared untenable.

It is worth dwelling on the difficulties of that period, for England and Robson. The tabloid media circulation war led to increasingly hyperbolic headlines about the manager's incapabilities (The *Mirror*'s "In the name of Allah, go" the most infamous). The English game's reputation for hooliganism and the growing mistrust between authorities and working-class supporters also threatened to overshadow the national team playing in the middle of it all.

On top of everything else, England were playing unadventurous, uninspiring football that reached a nadir with three straight goalless draws against Sweden, Poland and Italy. Robson's England were defensively sound (they didn't concede a single goal in 1990 World Cup qualifying) but he stood accused of starving the attack and so placing a low ceiling on England's natural talent.

It is a testament to Robson's character that he remained dignified in the face of such rampant media criticism, but his end became inevitable. With his England contract due to expire in January 1991 and with an offer from PSV Eindhoven on the table to fill their vacant managerial post following the 1990 World Cup, the story leaked and Robson was again hounded by a media that labelled him "a liar and a cheat" – two accusations that could not have been directed at a less deserving target. It was little surprise when Robson eventually signed the contract to leave his position after eight years in charge. For the second time in three World Cups, England's manager would leave immediately after it.

———

The 31 days between June 8 and July 8, 1990 were perceived – and not just in hindsight – as English football's Enlightenment. This was the first time an England team had reached the World Cup semi-final on foreign soil, when for a few precious days we truly did believe. For those four and a half weeks, a global sporting event was played out in glorious technicolour and can probably be called the start of the modern era of football.

If our eyes were opened to the possibility of footballing multiculturalism, Italia 90 also resold the image of English football and the English football supporter. The government, still led by Margaret Thatcher, had considered withdrawing the national team over concerns that it would become a "natural focus" for hooliganism.

Instead, the travelling hordes made their country as proud as their players did. There were impromptu kickabouts in town squares, late-night parties to celebrate good results and forget bad ones. The tournament did not pass without trouble, but the behaviour of England supporters was appreciated by the Italians.

Robson's squad of 22 players also helped to alter preconceptions. Only two outfielders in the squad were aged 30 or over and, while they rather limped through the group stages, England were the top scorers in the knockout stages. FIFA's technical report on the tournament noted the team's "ability to adapt and improvise with each other away from their league clubs".

The poster boy for this feel-good wave was Paul Gascoigne – "Gazza" – a young Geordie with a glint in his eye and magic in his feet. England's most junior player at Italia 90 was also their best. If an entire country came of age over those 31 days, a young central midfielder became a man, and a man became a superstar.

There were missteps, of course. The group stage was painful at times, qualification only secured through a Mark Wright header

Opposite above: Republic of Ireland players jump in celebration at Ray Houghton's winning goal against England at Euro 88.

Opposite below: Dutch striker Marco van Basten celebrates the first of his three goals against England in Düsseldorf. England lost all three games at Euro 88.

"I IMMEDIATELY KNEW IT WAS A HANDBALL AND I WAITED FOR THE OFFICIALS TO SORT IT OUT."

BOBBY ROBSON ON THAT INFAMOUS DIEGO MARADONA GOAL

against Egypt that was England's second goal of the tournament. But England grew into the World Cup and rose up to meet the rising expectations rather than shying away from them. That feat was achieved through a relaxed team spirit that never once veered into complacency, overseen by the avuncularity and warmth of spirit that came naturally to Robson.

Of course Italia 90 ended in heartbreak for England, just as every tournament that a team does not win must do. England were the better side in normal time against West Germany in their semi-final and, although the West Germans dominated extra time, David Platt had a goal ruled out for offside that was incredibly tight. But even disappointment came wrapped in a blanket of positivity. That Robson's team were even in a position to suffer such a defeat was sold as proof of their progress.

The 1990 World Cup did more than show off the flair and determination of England's players; it exhibited their vulnerabilities too. Before then, the archetypal British footballer was split into two obvious stereotypes. First came the clean-cut local boy made good, with stiff upper lip at times of crisis and humility when success came their way. The other was the bulldog, the hard-as-nails defender or midfielder who was prepared to run through walls for his country and then show off the bruises in the bar after the game. The defining image of England's qualification campaign for Italia 90 was not a Gary Lineker goal or a piece of John Barnes or Gascoigne skill, but blood

pouring from the head of Terry Butcher after receiving impromptu stitches to a deep cut against Sweden. Hard-wired machismo dictated that you had to be tough in order to thrive. Only the strongest will survive. Displaying emotion was to display weakness.

All that changed over the course of three hours on the evening of July 4 in Turin's Stadio delle Alpi. The tears shed by Gascoigne and Stuart Pearce, broadcast to 26.2 million people watching back home, affected us. We reacted not only on a sporting level, worried that Gascoigne missing the final would hurt England and Pearce's penalty miss would see us eliminated, but on a human level, too. The team returned to England with Robson's reputation enhanced, Gascoigne's place as an England cult hero established, Lineker's standing as England's best striker in a generation confirmed, and the national team closer to the country's hearts than it had been since 1970.

Opposite above: David Platt celebrates wildly after scoring an extra-time volley that would take England to the World Cup quarter-finals in 1990.

Opposite below: England supporters cheer on the team at Italia 90. The tournament saw the reputation of English football supporters abroad shift significantly; so too did Europe's opinion of the team.

Above: Bobby Robson and Paul Gascoigne embrace after England beat Cameroon to reach the World Cup semi-final in 1990 (left); and Robson and team doctor John Crane console a distraught Gascoigne after his yellow card in the 1990 World Cup semi-final (right).

PROFILE:
GARY LINEKER

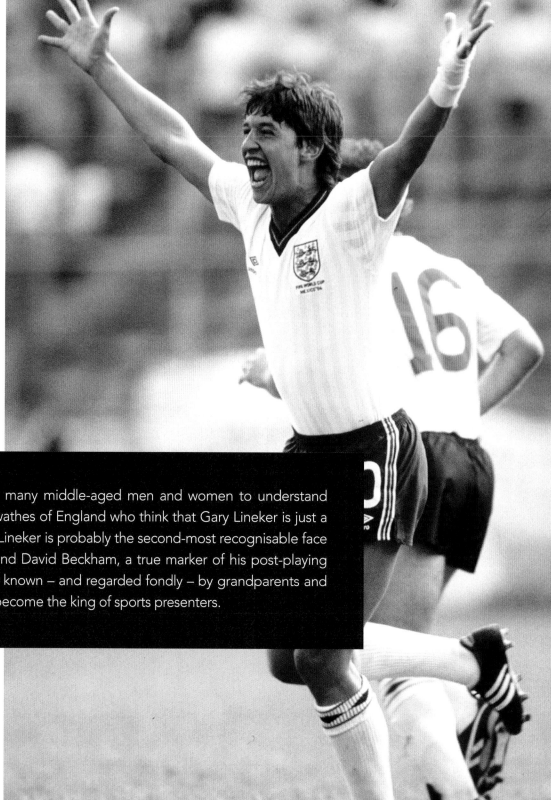

It might be hard for many middle-aged men and women to understand that there are vast swathes of England who think that Gary Lineker is just a television presenter. Lineker is probably the second-most recognisable face in English sport behind David Beckham, a true marker of his post-playing career success. He is known – and regarded fondly – by grandparents and grandsons, and has become the king of sports presenters.

But long before becoming the ubiquitous face of British sports coverage, Lineker was a national sporting hero. When he retired from international football in 1992, he was England's second-highest goalscorer (in 26 fewer caps than the great Bobby Charlton) and the only Englishman to win the Golden Boot at a World Cup. He has been overtaken by Wayne Rooney by the first measure and matched by Harry Kane on the second, but neither of those achievements undermine Lineker's legacy.

Lineker was one of English football's last great poachers. He was a penalty box predator with an astonishingly high conversion rate, largely because he took his shots from so close to goal. If you watch his 48 international goals, you can see how many were within 10 yards of the goal and how many were taken with his first touch of the move. Each of his six goals at the 1986 World Cup were taken from inside the six-yard box, including a hat-trick against Poland that was a first for England at a major tournament since the 1966 World Cup Final.

The temptation is to conclude that Lineker was merely hanging around the goalmouth, but he believed that to be an oversimplification of his game. "Everybody says it's being in the right place at the right time. But it's more than that; it's being in the right place all the time," he said, when asked about the art of being a centre-forward. "If I make 20 runs to the near post and each time I lose my defender, and 19 times the ball goes over my head or behind me – then one time I'm three yards out, the ball comes to the right place and I tap it in – then people say 'right place, right time'. And I was there all the time."

That all sounds very simple but the reality is far different. If many of Lineker's finishes were easy, with many amateur players confident of replicating them, getting to that right place was anything but. The difficulty lies in finding space, losing your marker, anticipating where the pass will be played and timing your run perfectly to meet it before an opponent detects your movement. That becomes harder as your career progresses because every defender knows exactly what you are trying to do. Lineker was like an actor delivering the perfect soliloquy on stage after months of learning their lines and perfecting their intonation and diction.

The last two decades has marked the rise of the multifunctional striker, expected to hold up the ball and bring others into play, drift wide to create space for onrushing midfielders and create chances as well as finish them. It's hard to see how Lineker would adapt to that. As England teammate Bryan Robson wrote in his autobiography:

Opposite: Gary Lineker rejoices after scoring his opening goal against Poland in the 1986 World Cup. He would complete his hat-trick, England's first at a World Cup since Geoff Hurst in 1966.

Above, from left: Lineker heads in England's goal against Argentina in the World Cup quarter-final in 1986 (left); and he celebrates with Terry Butcher (left) and Bryan Robson after a wonderful 4–2 friendly win in Spain in 1987.

Below: Lineker scores his fourth goal of the night against Spain, reinforcing his reputation as one of the best strikers in the world.

"Gary was an out-and-out finisher. He made no bones about it. He used to tell us, 'I'm not getting involved in any of that physical stuff. Just give me the ball and I'll score.' More often than not, he did."

But that should not be interpreted as anything other than a compliment. Lineker made it work because he was so supremely good at making life easier for those tasked with servicing him, and he barely let those standards slip. Between 1982 and 1992, he scored 207 goals in 339 league games despite never playing for the dominant club in the league and never winning a league title.

Lineker was also a relatively late bloomer. He was 23 before he started regularly in the First Division and had turned 24 before scoring his first England goal. That makes his eventual haul all the more impressive. Between 1985 and 1990, Lineker enjoyed a monumental half decade: three times top scorer in the First Division, three Player of the Year awards, a World Cup Golden Boot and a second place in the Ballon d'Or.

Almost as famous as Lineker's goalscoring record was his reputation for fair play. He is one of very few players of the last 40 years to have gone his entire career without being shown a yellow or red card. The closest he came was when playing in La Liga. "I almost got booked for grinning at a ref in Spain," Lineker told *FourFourTwo* magazine. "He actually warned me, 'Stop smiling,' and started to go for his pocket." If any footballer could be punished for being too pleasant, it is Lineker.

The only lingering regret is that Lineker's England career was comparatively short. Wayne Rooney's 53 goals were scored over a 13-year period, Bobby Charlton's over 12 years. Lineker's first came against the Republic of Ireland in 1985 and his last was scored against the CIS (formerly the Soviet Union) in 1992. Still, Lineker certainly made the most of his time in the sun. No player in the last 50 years has scored more World Cup goals in as few matches.

Leave it to Bobby Robson, a man who had an unerring ability to perfectly capture a person with a few simple words. After World Cup 86, England's manager was asked for his thoughts on Lineker's achievements with England. "He was everything I had hoped for," was Robson's reply. An entire nation nodded in agreement.

Opposite: Lineker celebrates after scoring the equaliser against West Germany in the 1990 World Cup semi-final.

Above: Lineker's shot past the despairing dive of Jürgen Kohler gives England hope, but penalties were to be their undoing.

Below: Lineker receives his OBE in March 1992 with then wife Michelle. He retired as England's second highest goalscorer.

CHAPTER ELEVEN

THE IMPOSSIBLE JOB?

1990–1996

WITH SIR BOBBY ROBSON HEADING TO EINDHOVEN, THE FA WERE LOOKING FOR THEIR FIRST NEW MANAGER IN ALMOST A DECADE. JOE ROYLE OF OLDHAM ATHLETIC AND HOWARD KENDALL OF MANCHESTER CITY (AND FORMERLY EVERTON) WERE BOTH CONSIDERED TO BE SERIOUS CANDIDATES, BUT GRAHAM TAYLOR WAS THE ONE WHO REALLY STOOD OUT. HIS APPOINTMENT WAS MET WITH WIDE APPLAUSE FROM SUPPORTERS AND THE MEDIA.

Taylor certainly had the CV to match the position. He had never played in the First Division or won a major trophy, but he had led Lincoln City to the Fourth Division title at the age of 28, took Watford from the fourth tier to second place in the First Division and the FA Cup Final in the space of six seasons. He had also led Aston Villa out of the Second Division to become a force in the First. Crucially, he had also worked with England's 'B' team and Under-21 side.

Given the circumstances in which Taylor ultimately left his position as England manager, it is tempting to assume that worrying cracks appeared from the start. In fact, the opposite is true. England became relentlessly efficient during Taylor's first two years in charge, losing only one of his first 21 matches in charge (1–0 against world champions West Germany). If there were doubts about England's functional style – they scored only seven goals in six qualifying matches for Euro 92 – Taylor's England were defensively solid and that was viewed in a positive light heading into a major tournament. After all, that had been the key to Robson's success in Italy.

England's group-stage exit at Euro 92 was certainly a significant setback for Taylor. The style of England's football was attacked by supporters, who pointed to England's record of 13 goals in their 13 games between September 1991 and the end of Euro 92. If that same charge was occasionally levelled against Bobby Robson's England, that team at least achieved in a major tournament. It was the lack of progress and style, in combination, that made Taylor so ripe for criticism.

England's Euro 92 exit provoked a wave of intense tabloid mania that, ultimately, Taylor was never able to overturn. The infamous "Swedes 2–1 Turnips" headline, mocking up England's manager as a vegetable, went far beyond the line of decency. "English football RIP" was another, coming days after several newspapers had talked up England's chances of winning the tournament. Like Robson before him, Taylor was the unwilling victim of a tabloid circulation war.

But he could also consider himself a little unfortunate. Injuries to Mark Wright, Paul Gascoigne and John Barnes hampered both England's defensive might and their creative threat. They were drawn in a tough group alongside France, eventual winners Denmark and tournament hosts Sweden, and held a half-time lead in their final group game that would have set up another semi-final against Germany.

———

The personnel at Taylor's disposal were also not conducive to major tournament success. There was an argument that England's manager moved Bryan Robson, Peter Beardsley and Chris Waddle to the fringes too quickly after the 1990 World Cup, but the two First Division title winners in 1992 and 1993 had a clutch of non-English key players: Gordon Strachan, Gary Speed, Gary Kelly, Gary McAllister and Eric Cantona for Leeds; Cantona, Peter Schmeichel, Ryan Giggs, Andrei Kanchelskis and Mark Hughes for Manchester United.

Taylor's biggest gripe surrounded the condition of the players that headed to Sweden. He was certain that a long, physically draining domestic season had fatigued his players, and believed changes were required if England were going to fulfil their potential when playing summer tournament football. Taylor was not alone; the club vs country argument stretched back at least as far as Don Revie's time in charge. Revie believed that he was hamstrung by the limitations of bureaucracy and the inability to rearrange domestic fixtures to benefit the England team. Almost 20 years later, Taylor believed little had changed.

That was one of the justifications for the formation of the Premier League, an idea mooted by the FA in their *Blueprint for the Future of Football* study, released in April 1991. Its aims were to increase playing standards, attract outside investment, improve the entertainment and facilities on offer and so promote the improvement of the England national team. The Premier League's formation was evidently controversial, but the FA believed the urgent need for progress on and off the field made the biggest constitutional change in English football history necessary.

The irony for Taylor is that the changes that he believed were necessary to improve the potential of the England team eventually created expectations that he was not able to meet. The formation and inauguration of the Premier League did not change the style of English football or even the quality of the players within the league overnight (there were just 13 foreign players present on its opening weekend, the majority of them Scandinavian), but it did broaden the nation's view of what might be possible and, most likely, created a subconscious demand for an England team that represented this new age.

Taylor's football had never aimed to be aesthetically pleasing. But when England were handed a daunting qualifying group for the 1994 World Cup, containing a nascent Norwegian team and a Dutch side that had finished ahead of Germany in their group at Euro 92, Taylor must have been worried. All the while, the scrutiny of the written press continued unabated.

Opposite: England manager Graham Taylor and assistant Lawrie McMenemy walk out for the second half of Taylor's first game in charge, a 1–0 win over Hungary at Wembley Stadium.

Above: England's players celebrate Gary Lineker's winner against Hungary in Taylor's first match in charge in September 1990.

Below: Paul Gascoigne dribbles past Balázs Berczy's desperate challenge during England's win over Hungary. Six months later, Gascoigne would suffer his first serious injury at the same stadium.

Here too, Taylor could reasonably claim a good deal of misfortune. England were let down by two dreadful refereeing decisions in their two group matches against the Netherlands: Jan Wouters went unpunished for using an elbow that fractured Paul Gascoigne's cheekbone, and Ronald Koeman was inexplicably not sent off for his last-man foul on David Platt. To make matters worse, the referee gave a free-kick, despite the offence continuing into the penalty area. Koeman then infamously went on to score his own free-kick later in the match.

But Taylor could only use poor luck as a partial defence. England drew against Poland and Norway at home, then lost in Oslo in the reverse fixture against the Norwegians. England scored 26 times in 10 qualifiers, a vast improvement on Euro 92 qualifying, but 19 of those goals came against San Marino and Turkey. They also lost the defensive solidity they had boasted heading into the European Championship, famously conceding after just eight seconds against San Marino.

Taylor was not a successful England manager, but he was a very decent man who was immensely proud to have been afforded the opportunity to lead his country. If his tactical leanings seemed to be at odds with the hype and excitement of the new Premier League era, they had previously (and subsequently) served him extremely well in the club game. A mix of injuries, a necessary squad overhaul, questionable decisions and missed chances at key moments of key matches undermined any hopes of sufficient progress. So in 1994, for the first time in 16 years, England would not be present at the World Cup.

Terry Venables was a relative outsider when the initial list of candidates to replace Taylor were rumoured. Don Howe was one option, but so too were the managers of Crystal Palace (Steve Coppell), Leeds United (Howard Wilkinson) and Queens Park Rangers (Gerry Francis). Venables had won the La Liga title and reached the European Cup Final with Barcelona before winning the FA Cup with Tottenham in 1991, and had been favourite at one stage to succeed Sir Bobby Robson. His warm relationship with Gascoigne was also seen as a major advantage in getting the best out of England's most talented player.

Venables inherited the unusual situation of facing England's longest run in peacetime history without a competitive match. Although the failure to qualify for World Cup 94 was a significant blow to England's hopes of kicking on after Italia 90, it did allow Venables to effectively build a team from scratch. In 1994 alone (Venables officially began

Above: England players close down French striker Eric Cantona during their 2–0 friendly win in February 1992.

Opposite above: Basile Boli challenges Alan Shearer during England's win. Shearer was making his international debut and scored.

Opposite below: Shearer and Lineker, both scorers against France, celebrate together. The pair would start only two games together for England, but both starred for their country at major tournaments.

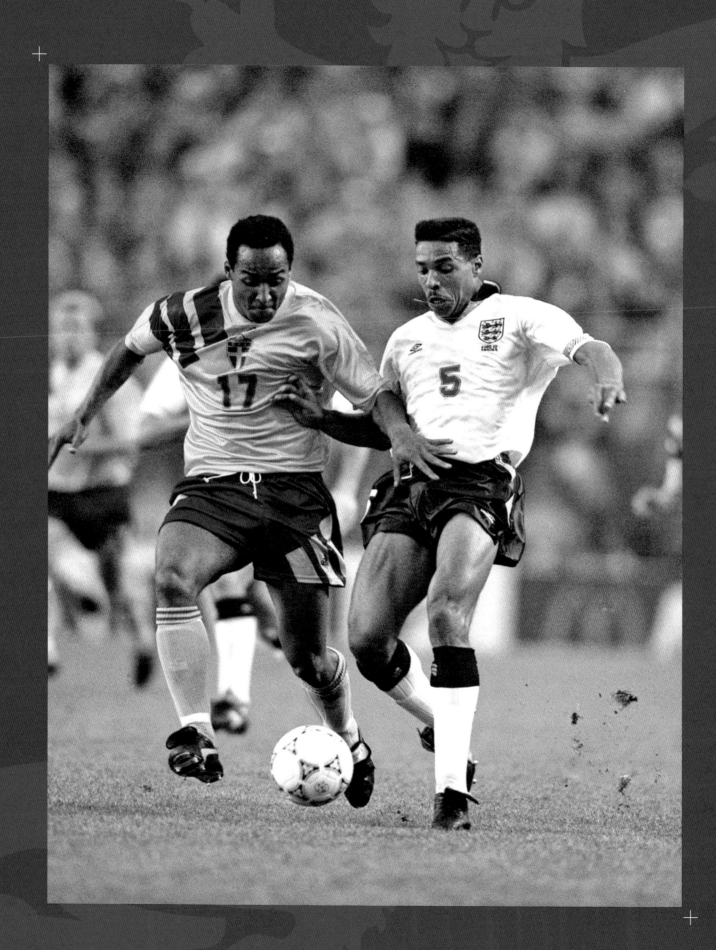

Opposite: England's Des Walker challenges Sweden's Martin Dahlin in the Euro 92 group game between the two countries.

Above: Gary Lineker is fouled by Sweden's Patrik Andersson. Lineker was controversially substituted and never scored for England again.

Below: Sweden's Tomas Brolin celebrates scoring the winner against England. Graham Taylor's side needed to win their final group match to qualify for the semi-finals.

"KEY TO VENABLES' PLAN TO RING THE CHANGES, BLOOD YOUNG PLAYERS AND CREATE A MERITOCRACY IN THE TEAM THAT HE BELIEVED WOULD CREATE HIGH COMPETITION FOR PLACES WAS THE EMERGING GENERATION OF DOMESTIC TALENT."

Above: Gary Lineker's substitution in the 61st minute against Sweden. It was to be his final cap for England.

Below and opposite: England's David Platt is fouled by Ronald Koeman of the Netherlands, who is not shown a red card by referee Karl Josef Assenmacher and a free-kick is awarded rather than a penalty. Koeman subsequently scored the opening goal of the game.

in the role in the January), nine new caps were awarded and 11 more followed in 1995.

England's new manager started by rebuilding the defence. Tony Adams, left at home in both 1990 and 1992, would be the mainstay. Gary Neville made his England debut in June 1995 and became a fixture at right-back. Next to Adams, Gareth Southgate won his first cap in December 1995. On the left, Stuart Pearce and Graeme Le Saux often rotated. David Seaman was Venables' first-choice goalkeeper. Seaman had made his debut as early as 1988, but had only made five competitive starts until Venables took over – he would end with 75 caps.

Key to Venables' plan to ring the changes, blood young players and create a meritocracy in the team that he believed would create high competition for places was the emerging generation of domestic talent. On October 1, 1995, the Neville brothers, Nicky Butt, Paul Scholes and David Beckham all played in the same Manchester United team in the Premier League for the first time. In the Liverpool side that faced them were Steve McManaman, Jamie Redknapp and Robbie Fowler, aged 23, 22 and 20 respectively.

If Venables understood the need to overhaul England's defence, the strikers rather took care of themselves. Never before can England have had such strength in depth in a single position as with their mid-1990s centre-forwards. In 1994–95, Alan Shearer, Fowler, Les Ferdinand, Stan Collymore and Andrew Cole were the top five goalscorers in the Premier League. If that group wasn't enough to cause selection headaches, Matthew Le Tissier, Teddy Sheringham and Ian Wright all also scored 18 or more league goals.

And there was a far greater reason for national anticipation and excitement. The FA had joined Austria, Greece, the Netherlands and Portugal in submitting bids to host the European Championship in 1996 and, in May 1992, England were given the honour of being hosts. For the first time since the glorious summer of 1966, England would be home to a major tournament. Logic dictated that this was our best chance of triumph in 30 years. Football, we would later learn, was coming home.

Above: England concede their quickest ever goal. Davide Gualtieri of San Marino scored past David Seaman after just eight seconds of their World Cup qualifier.

Below: The Premier League was launched in August 1992, with the explicit intention of increasing the time England managers got to spend with their players.

Opposite: Manchester United's Steve Bruce (left) and Bryan Robson (right) hold up the first ever Premier League trophy, won by Manchester United.

EURO 96:
FOOTBALL'S COMING HOME

In Nottingham, Croatia supporters wore their chequerboard shirts like a uniform, often using oversized flags as capes; they sang and danced in the city's pubs and bars. In Leeds, a 3.7m (12ft) football was erected in Victoria Gardens, French supporters posed for photographs in campsites on the edge of the city and Denmark trained on the Leeds Metropolitan University pitches at Weetwood. Liverpool was swamped by Russian supporters, while the city witnessed the improbable rise of a Czech Republic team that beat Italy at Anfield.

cross the country, 'Three Lions' played on loop, the new national anthem for a feel-good summer and beyond. We dreamt of Paul Gascoigne, Alan Shearer, David Seaman and Stuart Pearce composing new verse lyrics in real time and had those dreams realised, for better and for worse. Football had come home for the first time since 1966 and who knew when it would return again. England was determined to enjoy it.

Euro 96 was the first major international tournament held in Europe in the Premier League era. That mattered. For the first time, we watched foreign players not just within a temporary bubble of tournament intrigue but in anticipation that they might end up calling England home. Fourteen non-English goalscorers at the tournament would later play in the Premier League, with five – Karel Poborsky and Jordi Cruyff (Manchester United), Patrik Berger (Liverpool), Allan Nielsen (Tottenham) and Florin Răducioiu (West Ham) – arriving in the same year. The Premier League had the wealth to fund a foreign invasion and it was welcomed with open arms.

It was also a breakout summer for England, which defined Euro 96's legacy in this country. The intense, lingering disappointment suffered at Euro 92 and during qualification for the 1994 World Cup had dried up the goodwill garnered during Italia 90. Hosting the tournament provided England with a chance for success that the team grabbed with both hands, but it was also England's first competitive football for almost three years. Euro 96 was able to fill the vacuum created by that long absence.

England's campaign began in ignominy and media frenzy. A night out in Hong Kong on a pre-tournament tour had included predictable revelry but photographs had been sold to British tabloid newspapers, leading to a front-page scandal. When reports surfaced of further disorder on the Cathay Pacific flight that brought them back to London, there were vociferous calls for Gascoigne, one of the ringleaders, to be dropped from the squad.

Opposite: Stuart Pearce roars with relief after scoring his penalty against Spain in the quarter-finals, thus exorcising his demons of Italia 90.

Above: Tony Adams battles with Switzerland's Johann Vogel during the opening game of Euro 96 at Wembley.

Below: A group of England supporters pose for the cameras outside Wembley ahead of England's quarter-final against Spain.

" "IT JUST GALVANISED
US ALL TOGETHER AND
IT WAS ALMOST LIKE A
SIEGE MENTALITY – IT
WASN'T JUST US AGAINST
THE REST OF EUROPE BUT
AGAINST EVERYONE."

LES FERDINAND ON THE MEDIA
FRENZY BEFORE EURO 96

"

And yet the media furore became helpful to England. The squad decided to take the blame as one rather than let individuals be castigated and disciplined. "It really brought us together," Les Ferdinand later said. "There was always a feeling with England that whenever we got to a major competition the media always seemed to be against us, for one reason or another. It just galvanised us all together and it was almost like a siege mentality – it wasn't just us against the rest of Europe but against everyone."

In hindsight, Terry Venables' squad contained the perfect blend of youth and experience. Half of the 22-man tournament squad were aged 24 or under, including four – Sol Campbell, Robbie Fowler, and Gary and Phil Neville – who had not yet turned 22. But they were accompanied by older heads with major tournament experience: Gascoigne, captain Tony Adams, David Platt, Seaman and Pearce were all aged 29 or above.

Venables, parachuted into the job after the departure of Graham Taylor, understood the importance of creating a welcoming culture within the group that would be so vital for relieving the inevitable pressure of a home tournament. Friendly results had been mixed but, unusually, England peaked at a major tournament rather than before it.

The links with the 1966 World Cup were obvious: England disappointed in their opening matches, causing a wave of angst among the media and an expectant public. But everything seemed to change with Gascoigne's fabulous goal against Scotland at Wembley – surely England's best-ever tournament goal – and the playfully provocative celebration that followed it. This team were at their best when having fun; fun they would have.

Alan Shearer reignited his England career over the course of four weeks. His England form had dipped from patchy to non-existent, without an international goal in 12 appearances and almost two years. But Shearer scored in each of England's three group matches and against Germany in the semi-finals. He began the tournament with five international goals; four years later he would retire from international duty with 30.

Opposite: Paul Gascoigne volleys home one of England's most iconic goals to give his side a 2–0 lead over Scotland at Wembley.

Around Shearer's prolificacy, a series of legacy-creating moments arose. Gascoigne's goal against Scotland was coupled with his agonising slide in extra time against Germany. Shearer's lashed finish against Holland in the crushing 4–1 win was assisted by a piece of fantastic selflessness from Teddy Sheringham. Stuart Pearce scored his penalty against Spain to exorcise the demons of 1990 and celebrate with a passion unmatched by any supporter, either at Wembley or bursting with patriotic pride in their living rooms at home. And England, for the first time ever at a major tournament, won on penalties. On that point, heartache was just around the corner. You can't have everything.

England also rode their luck. The draw with Switzerland was lethargic. Gary McAllister's penalty miss for Scotland was an assist for Gascoigne's goal. The quarter-final with Spain was a nervous, uncomfortable experience from which England were fortunate to escape – a penalty decision went England's way, a Spain "offside" goal was disallowed, and several excellent saves were needed from Seaman for the team to survive and reach penalties. Without all of those things tipping in England's favour, 1996 would not be remembered as fondly.

But then they did survive them; that was entirely the point. England hoped, England stumbled, England surged on and England delivered. Euro 96 was a hypnotic tournament, not because of the quality of its football or because England triumphed in the final, but because it captured the national mood – Cool Britannia, a new hope, a new age for society – by mirroring it.

If the nightmarish image of Gareth Southgate's missed penalty was etched in the English sporting memory long after the Croatians, Russians, French and Czechs had left our cities comparatively silent, that didn't matter. The England team had won back the love of its public once again.

Above, top: Alan Shearer lashes the ball past Edwin van der Sar to give England a 3–1 lead over the Netherlands in their final group match.

Above: Shearer celebrates against the Dutch. He would end Euro 96 as the tournament's top scorer with five goals.

Opposite: A forlorn Gareth Southgate trudges away from his missed penalty against Germany in the semi-final penalty shoot-out.

CHAPTER TWELVE

REAGAN'S TIME

1980s

WHEN TOMMY TRANTER STEPPED DOWN FROM HIS POSITION AS MANAGER OF THE ENGLAND WOMEN'S TEAM EARLY IN 1979, THE FA WERE TASKED WITH FINDING A LONG-TERM REPLACEMENT. THEY INITIALLY ASKED JOHN SIMS TO STAND IN AS CARETAKER AHEAD OF AN UNOFFICIAL EUROPEAN TOURNAMENT IN ITALY, AT WHICH ENGLAND BEAT FINLAND AND SWITZERLAND BEFORE LOSING 2–1 TO ITALY IN THE SEMI-FINALS. WITH SIMS THEN MOVING ON AS PLANNED, FA COACH MIKE RAWDING TOOK CHARGE OF A FRIENDLY AGAINST DENMARK THAT MARKED THE 10-YEAR ANNIVERSARY OF THE WOMEN'S FOOTBALL ASSOCIATION.

But their permanent choice was Martin Reagan, a mild-mannered coach who would become beloved by the players he developed during his 12 years in the role. After his death in 2016 at the age of 92, Marieanne Spacey, one of England's greatest-ever forwards, described him as, "a gentleman from whom everyone that came into contact with him walked away smiling".

Hope Powell, given her England debut by Reagan at the age of 16 (and eventually becoming England manager), was just as effusive with her praise. "Martin was a real gentleman and a lovely human being," she said. "He tried to move the women's game forward at a time when resources were minimal. He did his job for the love of the game and made the best of what we had at the time."

Reagan had been a coach within the FA's system for 25 years, following a playing career that included spells at Hull City, Middlesbrough, Portsmouth and Norwich City. But he was far more than a former footballer. On October 20, 1944, as Sergeant Tank Commander in 204 Armoured Assault Squadron, Royal Engineers, he rescued survivors from an explosion in Normandy that killed 40 British and Canadian soldiers. England's new coach was also the recipient of the French Legion of Honour.

Right: Match poster for England's friendly against Norway in October 1981, held at Cambridge United's Abbey Stadium. Norway won the match 3–0.

Opposite, from top: Linda Curl preparing for England training in February 1986; Debbie Bampton during England's 6–0 European Competition for Women qualifier against the Republic of Ireland in September 1983 (top right); and Brenda Sempare during the same fixture. England topped their group, winning all six qualifiers.

NORWICH BREWERY *Presents*
LADIES
INTERNATIONAL FOOTBALL
ENGLAND
V
NORWAY
at the ABBEY STADIUM, CAMBRIDGE
SUNDAY OCTOBER 25th 1981
KICK-OFF 3.15 pm
PLUS ~ *ENTERTAINMENT FROM 2.30 BY*
THE DAGENHAM DRUM CORPS
British Drum Corp Champions
All Proceeds from the Match to the
NORWICH BREWERY SPORTING FUND
in association with the
SPORTS AID FOUNDATION
PRESENTATIONS at HALF TIME BY
DAVE `BOY`GREEN
ADMISSION: ADULTS £1.00 CHILDREN/O.A.Ps 50p
GATES OPEN 2.00 pm

By kind permission of
CAMBRIDGE UNITED FOOTBALL CLUB

As with his predecessors, life as England manager was not easy for Reagan. Resources were scant, with players recalling having to sleep on the floor of a gym before one international friendly. Reagan's training was notoriously fitness-based, the squad joking in hindsight about the fear of his circuit training drills that consisted of press-ups, sit-ups and burpees. You could take the man out of the military, but the military stayed within the man.

But Reagan was left with little choice. The England squad would typically meet up on a Friday night before a match on a Sunday. Most managers in those circumstances would prefer to focus on the opposition's likely tactics, but that information simply wasn't available. There were no scouts to provide reports, no blanket TV or radio coverage to allow Reagan to work on a specific plan for each match. Sometimes that helped England – they simply concentrated on perfecting their own game – but occasionally opponents produced tactical surprises that the manager really needed to be aware of in advance.

If life as an England player on international duty was difficult, the squad was used to hardship. In her autobiography, Powell discussed being perpetually short of money because she had to pay her own way in the domestic game. While at Millwall Lionesses, players raised money through raffles, social events and begging letters to potential sponsors for training kits, match balls, pitch hire and match fees. Powell and her colleagues all worked full-time or, just as often, a series of part-time jobs that they could fit in around football.

In 1982, UEFA formally established a women's European Championship for the first time under the wordy title of UEFA European Competition for Representative Women's Teams, although with only 16 nations taking part in the first edition in 1984, fewer than half of UEFA's members, it could not be considered official. The tournament was split into two parts, a four-group qualifying stage that led to semi-finals and a final that were also held as two-legged, home and away ties.

Qualifying was decided on a regional basis, which undeniably helped England. Not only did they avoid Sweden and Italy – probably the

Above: England great Gillian Coultard in action against the Republic of Ireland in September 1983 at Elm Park, Reading.

Opposite: England's Kerry Davis runs with the ball during England's European Competition for Women qualifier against Northern Ireland in September 1982. England won the game 7–1.

two best teams in Europe – they were given games against Northern Ireland, Scotland and Ireland, making them overwhelming favourites in the Great Britain & Ireland group. England won all six of their qualifiers, scoring 24 times and conceding only once, in a 7–1 victory over Northern Ireland in their first game.

Drawn against Denmark in the semi-finals (the Danes had been placed in the Central group and so also avoided Sweden), England took a first-leg lead at Crewe Alexandra's Gresty Road stadium through Linda Curl and recovered immediately from an Inge Hindkjær strike to take a slender lead through Liz Deighan to Denmark. Three weeks later in Hjorring, Reagan's side produced a brilliant, battling performance to win 1–0 with Debbie Bampton scoring the winner late in the first half. Sweden had beaten Italy home and away in the other semi-final, Pia Sundhage scoring three times. England were about to face the best player in the world.

The first leg of the final in Sweden offered an opportune chance for England's players to witness how the other half lived. The two sides were well matched on the pitch but the difference in media coverage was night and day. The match was given hour-long highlights on Swedish television and covered extensively in the country's newspapers. The match was played in the Ullevi Stadium in Gothenburg, a 43,000-capacity ground that had hosted the European Cup Winners' Cup Final a year earlier. England were beaten 1–0 by a Sundhage goal, with goalkeeper Terry Wiseman making some fantastic saves to keep England in the contest.

England's home ground for the second leg became a bone of contention. Numerous league clubs were asked to provide facilities but declined, with Luton Town eventually offering Kenilworth Road. The pitch was boggy and virtually unfit for purpose, the crowd sparse and the media coverage almost non-existent. England's team did not wear the same kit as their male counterparts and the game existed inside the bubble of women's football, far outside the growing modernisation of the men's game.

England used the match-day programme to make their point. Not only did it list the players' names, numbers and positions, it included their full-time jobs too: office clerk (Carol Thomas), civil servant (Linda Curl), sales assistant (Brenda Sempare) and electronic engineer (Liz Deighan).

Within the programme, WFA secretary Linda Whitehead made a plea: "We hope that this will be the turning point for women's football in this country and that the players begin to get the recognition that they rightly deserve." To even be competing with Sweden, given their resources, was a triumph.

And England came so close to victory in that maiden championship. Wiseman was again at her best, making crucial saves either side of Curl's first-half goal that eventually produced the dreaded penalty shoot-out. There was heartbreak for Curl and Lorraine Hanson, who missed their penalties. The winning spot kick was taken and scored, fittingly, by Sundhage. But Sweden's players expressed their admiration for the performance of the England side.

For all the roadblocks put in the path of the England team at club level, this was a team with real talent. Pat Chapman was a skilful forward, ably assisted in the forward line by Curl or Kerry Davis. Bampton and Gillian Coultard were both excellent passing midfielders. Wiseman was the best goalkeeper at the tournament by some distance,

frequently keeping England in their semi-final and final after barely being required in the group stage.

What England lacked was a youth system that ensured the identification and development of the next generation. Before the tournament, Sweden had held a talent identification course for 350 girls aged 11 or 12. But within the education system, there were few opportunities for girls to even form a love of football, let alone play the game regularly and be coached to a high standard. Many of the England squad in 1984 had grown up playing in boys' teams, but that was not possible in the professional game.

In February 1987, the WFA appointed Liz Deighan, a midfielder in Reagan's 1984 Euros team, to the position of England Under-21 manager when a team for that age group was formed for the first time. Deighan would eventually be succeeded by John Bilton, but within five years the team had folded due to a lack of resources.

With the format of the UEFA European Competition for Representative Women's Teams yet to commit to a four-yearly cycle

Opposite, from top: England captain Carol Thomas shakes the hand of her counterpart ahead of their European Competition for Women final second leg at Luton's Kenilworth Road (top); Sweden's squad celebrate victory after their penalty shoot-out win. England won the second leg 1–0.

Above: The match programme for the final second leg. Kenilworth Road was used after a number of English teams refused to allow their pitch to be used for the game.

(that would come from 1997 onwards), England had tournaments in 1987 and 1989 to look forward to, with qualifying campaigns that would at least provide regular competitive football.

Qualifying was altered for the 1987 tournament, with Europe no longer divided into regional groups. Sweden were drawn alongside Belgium, France and the Netherlands, while 1984 semi-finalists Denmark faced a daunting task against emerging nation Norway. England, however, again formed part of a home nations group and found qualification just as easy as before. They scored 34 times in six group matches, including 7–1 and 10–0 wins over Northern Ireland.

In 1987, the draw for the final stages would not be as kind as before. With games being held in Norway and played over single legs, England were drawn to face Sweden in the final four, while new favourites Norway hosted Italy. England came close again to beating a higher quality team, taking the lead with two goals in eight minutes after Anette Börjesson's opener. But Gunilla Axen, a squad member in 1984, scored a second-half equaliser before adding a second in extra time as England could not resist intense Swedish pressure. A defeat in the third-place play-off to Italy, after again having taken the lead, was viewed as satisfactory but nothing more.

By 1989, regional qualification had been removed entirely and Reagan's team were handed an astonishingly hard task in a group containing previous semi-finalists Denmark and reigning champions Norway. Early victories in Finland and at home to Denmark at Blackburn Rovers' Ewood Park, combined with Norway dropping

points against Finland, offered hope of qualification. But England then lost 2–0 in Denmark, home and away against Norway and could only draw at home to Finland at Millwall's The Old Den. The Finland draw was disastrous; Norway topped the group and Denmark eliminated England on goal difference.

Even so, Reagan's record in charge of England was a proud one. He remained in place throughout the 1980s, often calling up teenagers in a bid to provide them with the kind of high-class opposition necessary to improve their technique and create familiar relationships among players. Everyone who worked and played under Reagan remarked on how diligently he tried to improve the environment in which a successful team could be created.

And Reagan was successful. Between June 1980 and the end of the decade, England played 51 matches and won 31 of them. Of their 11 defeats, nine came against Sweden, Norway and Denmark, proof that Scandinavia was leading the world in its commitment to the development of women's football. Other European nations with significant pedigrees in the men's game, including England, Germany and Italy, were playing catch-up.

But positive change was coming. In the late 1980s, a global boom in women's football began. Japan's first domestic league commenced in 1989, followed by the inaugural United States Interregional Women's League in the early 1990s. In the UK, there was a rapid rise in the participation of girls in sport both inside and outside the education system.

In 1988, FIFA Congress organised an international invitational tournament in China that was designed to gauge interest in a Women's World Cup, following the regular hosting of non-official tournaments such as the Women's World Invitational Tournament (1978–87) and the Mundialito (1981–88). Twelve national teams took part, with Europe, Asia, Africa, South America, North America and Oceania all represented.

The tournament was a huge success, with attendances averaging 20,000. More than 45,000 watched hosts China play Canada. By June 30, just 18 days after Norway had defeated Sweden in the final, FIFA approved the establishment of the first official FIFA Women's World Cup. No longer would women's international football have to exist in the shadows. Several superpowers were forming, investing heavily in the game's progression. England did not want to miss the party.

That party would take place without Reagan being invited. A 6–1 aggregate defeat to Germany in qualifying for the UEFA Women's Euro 1991 meant that England missed out on a place at the main tournament but also decreed that England would be absent from the inaugural World Cup held later the same year in China – nations would qualify directly from the Euro. Reagan was sacked in December 1990 and became a director of coaching at a soccer camp in California until his retirement.

Above: Marieanne Spacey celebrates her goal against the Republic of Ireland at Wembley in April 1988 during the Mercantile Credit Football Festival to celebrate 100 years of the Football League.

Opposite: Maria Harper during England's exhibition match against the Republic of Ireland at Wembley. England won 2–0 thanks to goals from Spacey and Gillian Coultard.

GILLIAN COULTARD

In January 2021, Gillian Coultard got the email that she had long given up hope of ever receiving. It explained that she was being awarded an MBE for services to football. Almost 20 years after her final England cap, and 14 years after her induction into the England football Hall of Fame, Coultard assumed that she had simply dropped through the cracks. She had never demanded nor expected recognition for her work, but that doesn't mean that such recognition was not merited.

When Coultard was born in 1963, the youngest of eight children in a town on the outskirts of Doncaster, a life in football could barely have been considered a possibility. England would not play their first official international until Coultard was nine years old. But Coultard loved the game. She played with the boys and fell in love with Doncaster Rovers. At the age of just 13, she joined Doncaster Belles and began a 24-year affiliation with her hometown club.

The sacrifices Coultard made to pursue that career should not be underestimated. She never earned money from playing the game, combining her career with a job on the production line at the Pioneer electronics factory in Castleford, and training four evenings a week. That took its toll. During the later part of her career, Coultard expressed her disappointment that the men's game allowed for full professionalism that would remain a pipe dream for her and her teammates.

Far from giving her a living, football cost her a lot of money in match fees and travel costs. She did it for love and because she believed that stopping playing would be to let down those around her whom she was proud to call her friends.

Coultard's affiliation to the Belles cost her a shot at monetising her talent. She bemoaned the poor set-up of women's football in England in comparison to Continental Europe, where players were routinely released from work commitments to accommodate their training schedules, or became full-time professionals. She also pointed out that it put England at a disadvantage in major competitions.

And Coultard did receive offers to move abroad, from Sweden, Italy and Belgium. She refused because she was understandably concerned that if those ventures were not successful, she would be forced to return to England without the security of the full-time employment she had sacrificed to take the plunge. Later in her career Coultard admitted she regretted that call, but there's no doubt it would have been a risk.

Those regrets, however, should not overshadow the extraordinary journey on which Coultard embarked, despite the many roadblocks she faced. At the Belles, she won two Women's Premier League titles and six FA Women's Cup trophies in over 300 appearances. In 1990, Coultard scored the only goal in the FA Women's Cup Final at Derby County's Baseball Ground as the Belles beat Friends of Fulham to lift their third title in four years.

One of the high points of Coultard's England career came on June 6, 1995, when England played their first ever World Cup match against Canada in Helsingborg, Sweden. In the 51st minute, with the score still 0–0, Karen Farley turned away from a Canadian defender and was fouled by Michelle Ring. When referee Eva Odlund pointed to the spot, 31-year-old Coultard picked up the ball and directed her penalty past Carla Chin, who got a touch on the ball but could not halt its progress. Forty-five years after England's men's team scored their first World Cup finals goal, Coultard scored the landmark goal for the women's team. Later in the same game, Coultard scored a header to give England a 3–0 lead, but she had given England's second penalty of the match to Marieanne Spacey, thus missing out on a famous hat-trick.

"I think it was a bit of a gas really, as if to say, let Marieanne take it rather than me, as mine only just got in," Coultard said. "When I look back at it and think I've scored the header as well, I could have been the first woman to get a hat-trick, but it wasn't to be!"

During her career, beginning in 1981 and ending in the first year of the 21st century, Coultard witnessed seismic change in women's football in England. In 1984 she started both legs of the final against Sweden in the inaugural European Competition for Women's Football. In 1991, she played in the opening weekend of the new Women's Football Association (WFA) National League – the Doncaster Belles were crowned as the first champions, winning all 14 of their league matches.

In 1997, the FA announced plans to develop the women's game at every level from grassroots to elite sport. That plan included the formation of centres of excellence around the country that would allow for the identification and development of talent to create pathways to an organised game, with leagues and cups working with sponsors to generate revenue to further aid the sport's expansion.

Coultard played a significant role. Having retired from England in 2000 and hung up her boots at Doncaster Belles in 2001, receiving a plaque for her service, she switched her focus to a coaching role at the National Women's Football Academy in Durham. At the age of 37, now was the time for her to pass on her wisdom and expertise to those girls who could use her as a phenomenal role model for their own careers.

That presents Coultard as more than a mere cog in the wheel in the development of women's football. At every step of the journey, she was a leading actor. At every stage in the overdue progress of the women's game, she was present in the red and white of the Belles or the all white of England. Coultard's career is of greater significance even than the trophies and plaudits she earned along the way; she runs like a vein through the expansion of the women's game, a statue to the dedication and sacrifice required for those who came after her to enjoy an easier, better and more rewarding professional life.

Opposite: Gillian Coultard playing for England against Romania in October 1998. Coultard scored twice in England's first ever Women's World Cup match against Canada.

Below: Coultard challenging for the ball against Scotland at Bramall Lane in March 1997. England won 1–0.

CHAPTER THIRTEEN

GOLDEN GENERATIONS

1996–2006

DURING THE MID-1990S, ENGLISH FOOTBALL UNDERWENT A REVOLUTION. THE RISE IN REVENUES LINKED TO BROADCASTING DEALS, INCREASING NUMBERS OF FOREIGN PLAYERS AND MANAGERS, AND AN IMPROVEMENT IN TRAINING AND DIET ALL CAUSED A SEISMIC JUMP IN PROFESSIONALISM. IF THE PREMIER LEAGUE HAD SIMPLY BEEN A REBADGED FIRST DIVISION IN ITS FORMATIVE YEARS, NOW IT WAS TRANSFORMED INTO A LEAGUE OF ITS OWN.

That produced a new breed of English league footballer, one that had developed under the watchful gaze of mentoring managers and players. At Manchester United, Eric Cantona led by example in training. At Arsenal, Arsène Wenger's appointment transformed both his club and the culture of the league as a whole, with Dennis Bergkamp his disciple on the pitch. At Chelsea, Ruud Gullit was first a culturally influential player, then manager. At Tottenham, Jürgen Klinsmann twice proved the value of combining impeccable conditioning with an unrelenting desire to win. At Newcastle, David Ginola's skill and flair offered a glimpse of a bright new future.

The FA, tasked with finding a new manager after Terry Venables had chosen to stand down after Euro 96, wanted to follow that lead. Venables had altered England's style from the defensive caution of the Taylor years and had aimed to play with flair. The FA required a manager with foreign coaching principles who was committed to a similar ideal. Glenn Hoddle was the obvious candidate.

After retiring as a brilliant, mercurial player, one of the most talented in England's history and who had felt misused and unfairly ignored by his international managers, Hoddle had taken Swindon Town up into the Premier League before joining Chelsea. His Premier League record at Stamford Bridge was a little patchy, but they had performed well in cup competitions. Hoddle had also created the most multinational league squad in England and preferred a continental, passing style.

He was also parachuted into an attractive position. The Manchester United academy graduates were ready to become international regulars, while Wenger had revitalised the careers of several of Arsenal's senior players. Newcastle United, Aston Villa and Nottingham Forest had emerged as unexpected, if not quite sustainable, domestic challengers with English players at their core.

Hoddle did not feel the need to rewrite Venables' script. He handed two players their debut in his first game in charge – David Beckham and Andy Hinchcliffe – but was generally reserved with his bestowal of new

caps. When new players did emerge, they tended to stick around: of the five England debutants in 1997, four (Rio Ferdinand, Paul Scholes, David James and Nicky Butt) would go on to amass 239 caps between them.

The new England manager's first task was to qualify for World Cup 98 after the bitter disappointment of 1994. With only one team qualifying automatically from each group (a second would face a play-off) and England facing Italy and Poland, it would not be easy. England started well, beating Moldova, Poland and Georgia, but lost to Italy at Wembley thanks to Gianfranco Zola's shot past stand-in goalkeeper Ian Walker.

Better form was to come. In the summer of 1997, England travelled to France for a World Cup warm-up, round-robin tournament against France, Italy and Brazil. They earned effusive praise for victories over the hosts and Italy, securing tournament victory before a 1–0 defeat to Brazil. That progress was assisted by Italian stumbles against Georgia and Poland, meaning England needed only a draw in Rome to top their qualifying group. After an authoritative, defensively secure performance (except for Christian Vieri's late missed header), England and Hoddle had completed their first task.

The 1998 World Cup provided only another major tournament "what if?" for England. They were comfortable winners over Colombia and Tunisia but were abject against Romania and so missed out on top spot in Group G. Rather than Croatia in Bordeaux, a tie for which England would have been favourites, they were drawn against Argentina in St Etienne. It would be the first competitive meeting between the two sides since the 1986 World Cup.

It was a controversial, and at times, bad-tempered match. England responded brilliantly to going behind, Michael Owen scoring perhaps the country's greatest-ever World Cup goal. But they were undone first by a pre-planned free-kick move, and then by David Beckham's

retaliation against Diego Simeone. England may well have won the game with 11 men and performed exceptionally well in adversity, but they were destined to lose on penalties again.

The public and media reaction was far more forgiving than usual, unless you happened to be Beckham. While Manchester United's No. 7 was vilified and cruelly taunted across the country, Hoddle's reputation had actually improved despite England's worst World Cup showing since 1958. Beckham would have his revenge, however, and earn the love and respect of his people.

And Hoddle, ultimately, would lose his job. Results in subsequent European Championship qualifying (drawing with Bulgaria and losing to Sweden) were underwhelming after the excitement and promise of France. Hoddle released a serialised World Cup autobiography that caused a huge stir in the FA and among his own squad. When an interview with *The Times* newspaper reflected aspects of Hoddle's religious views, his position became untenable. With Euro 2000 qualification to fight for, England were looking for a fifth manager in as many major tournaments.

Again, there was a clear public choice. Like Hoddle, Kevin Keegan was a former England fans' favourite with experience of playing abroad. Like Hoddle, he had taken a club up to the Premier League, but Keegan stayed at Newcastle and led them to two top-three finishes in as many years before resigning due to the ongoing psychological blow of missing out on the league title in 1996. In the process of

Opposite: Paul Ince is consoled by Glenn Hoddle after missing his penalty in the shoot-out against Argentina in the last 16 of the 1998 World Cup.

Above: David Batty's crucial penalty is saved by Argentinean goalkeeper Carlos Roa. For the third time in four major tournaments, England have lost on penalties.

 "THERE IS NOT A HUGE ABUNDANCE OF ENGLISH COACHES NOW. IF WE ARE GOING TO GET THE RIGHT MAN WE ARE GOING TO HAVE TO CAST THE NET WIDER. WE'LL GET THE RIGHT PERSON, WHATEVER THAT ENDS UP COSTING."

FA CHIEF EXECUTIVE ADAM CROZIER ON APPOINTING KEVIN KEEGAN'S SUCCESSOR

taking free-spending Fulham into the Premier League, Keegan initially took the England job alongside his Fulham work. That lasted only two months before he made it clear that England was his priority.

Keegan did not find it easy. He won his first game 3–1 against Poland, Scholes scoring a hat-trick, but drew with Hungary, Bulgaria and the return fixture against Poland. England finished nine points behind Sweden and only qualified for a play-off on goal difference. Their 2–0 first-leg victory over Scotland at Hampden Park should have made qualification certain but it only came after a nervy, disappointing 1–0 home defeat in the second leg.

Given the squad at Keegan's disposal, Euro 2000 represented one of England's biggest tournament disappointments. They had a core of very successful Manchester United players (Phil and Gary Neville, Beckham and Scholes), the experience of Paul Ince, Tony Adams, Alan Shearer and David Seaman, the world-class youngster Owen, and Steve McManaman, who had just won the Champions League with Real Madrid.

From the moment they went 2–0 up over Portugal in their first group game, England floundered. They were too cavalier given the comfort of their lead and eventually lost 3–2. They then beat a Germany side in a state of flux 1–0 and then lost 3–2 to Romania despite only requiring a draw and being 2–1 up at half-time. A painful exit was inflicted by a penalty again, but this time it came in normal time when Viorel Moldovan fired past Seaman in the last minute of their final match.

That was the beginning of a swift end for Keegan, who eventually resigned after the final match at the old Wembley Stadium, which then closed for rebuilding. Dietmar Hamann's free-kick consigned England to World Cup qualification defeat against Germany and

Keegan had had enough. He was a kind, well-meaning, optimistic man and manager, but suspicions had grown that the Newcastle United experience had broken his spirit.

If the Premier League's transformation across the 1990s was widely loved – increased entertainment, more televised matches, blanket media coverage, intriguing and inspiring foreign players – that revolution caused a decline in the fortunes of English managers. With foreign names now linked – and usually appointed – with every major club job, domestic options to replace Keegan were relatively scarce.

Most of the obvious contenders had already been given the chance and failed to match expectations. No English manager had won the Premier League and only one had won the FA Cup since the league's formation. Only three English managers had even finished in the top three (Roy Evans, Frank Clark and Ron Atkinson) and the highest-placed English manager in 1999–2000 was Aston Villa's John Gregory. None were seriously considered as candidates.

FA Chief Executive Adam Crozier conceded that an English appointment would be difficult: "There is not a huge abundance

Opposite above: David Beckham despairs as England lose 3–2 to Romania at Euro 2000 and are eliminated after the group stages.

Opposite below: Kevin Keegan leaves the Wembley pitch after England's home defeat to Germany in October 2000. Keegan would resign from his position shortly afterwards.

Above: Michael Owen is tackled by Germany's Dietmar Hamann in the World Cup qualifier at Wembley. Hamann's free-kick would be the only goal of the game.

of English coaches now. If we are going to get the right man we are going to have to cast the net wider. We'll get the right person, whatever that ends up costing."

And so England appointed the first foreign manager in its history and paid him £2m a year, making him the highest-paid football manager in the country, earning at least double the salary of any predecessor. It was a huge show of faith in Sven-Göran Eriksson, but then his CV demanded that faith. Here was a coach at the top of his game who had proven himself across Europe, domestically and in tournament competitions.

Some railed against it, believing that England's failure to stick with their own represented an inherent failure of patriotism. One columnist wrote that England had "sold our birthright down the river to a nation of seven million skiers and hammer-throwers who spend half their lives in darkness." Not only did that seem wildly melodramatic given the success of other nations with non-domestic managers, a mischievous response might be to point out that it was also inaccurate: no Swede had even entered qualifying for the hammer throw at the most recent Summer Olympics nor won a skiing gold at the Winter Games.

Eriksson's England tenure started at a gallop. Emphatic friendly victories over Spain (3–0) and Mexico (4–0) were interspersed with equally comfortable World Cup qualifying wins over Finland, Albania and Greece. Eriksson was acutely aware that automatic qualification depended upon victory in Munich and knew too that it was a daunting task. Germany had only lost one home qualifier in their history.

The night of September 1, 2001, turned out to be the most famous qualification victory in England's history. Eriksson's side conceded early but, rather than implode, they produced a mesmeric display of attacking football that ended in a monumental 5–1 win. If the margin of victory was a little flattering, the dominance of England's

Below: Michael Owen celebrates a goal against Germany. Owen scored three times in 54 minutes to maintain his reputation as one of the best young strikers in the world.

Right: The scoreboard in Munich's Olympiastadion displays England's dominance. The 5–1 defeat was only Germany's second ever loss in World Cup qualifying.

performance in adversity merited any fortune. When the great Franz Beckenbauer was asked for his thoughts on the old adversary, he did not try to hide his admiration: "I have never seen a better England team and I have never seen an England team playing better football. It was fantasy football with England on a high."

England, as was their custom, did eventually labour to World Cup qualification. But then that allowed Beckham to write the final chapter in the narrative of his national redemption, scoring a brilliant last-minute free-kick against Greece at Old Trafford, having dragged England back into the game. England were heading to Japan and South Korea without the need for a nervous play-off, something that appeared highly unlikely at the time of Eriksson's appointment.

In mournful hindsight, the 5-1 win in Germany was the high point of Eriksson's five-year tenure with England. At the World Cup the following summer, England were guilty of missed opportunities. They atoned for a tepid performance against Sweden with a 1–0 victory over Argentina, Beckham earning his revenge with the only goal, but a 0–0 draw with Nigeria was a huge misstep. Topping the group would have created a pathway to the semi-final against Senegal and

Left: Rio Ferdinand is congratulated after giving England the lead against Denmark in their last-16 tie at the 2002 World Cup.

Below: Michael Owen celebrates Ferdinand's goal. England would win the game 3–0 in one of their most complete World Cup performances in recent memory.

Opposite: David Beckham and Michael Owen embrace as England celebrate a goal against Denmark. The win set up a quarter-final against eventual champions Brazil.

Opposite: England's players celebrate Michael Owen's early
opener against Portugal in their Euro 2004 quarter-final.

Above: David Beckham sends his penalty over the bar after
slipping during the shoot-out against Portugal.

Below: Darius Vassell sees his penalty saved by Portugal goalkeeper
Ricardo, who then scored the winning spot kick to send Portugal through.

Turkey. Instead, England finished second and tamely lost to eventual champions Brazil in the quarter-finals, despite taking the lead.

Euro 2004 was a similar story. England did reach the quarter-finals, with Wayne Rooney replacing Michael Owen as the boy wonder story. But were it not for either of Zinedine Zidane's 91st and 93rd-minute goals in England's opening game, they would have faced a potential route of Greece and the Czech Republic to reach the final. Even in the tougher half of the draw, Rooney's first-half injury and a controversially disallowed Sol Campbell goal were decisive as England exited a major tournament on penalties for the third time in five attempts.

At World Cup 2006, Eriksson's last attempt at taking the country to glory, England reproduced all of its familiar major tournament dramas and flaws. There was the new kid on the block in the shape of Theo Walcott, a left-field selection who did not play a minute. There were the injuries: Gary Neville missed three matches with a calf strain and captain Beckham was forced off during the quarter-final against Portugal. There was the ill discipline, Rooney mirroring Beckham in 1998 by being sent off for the petulant stray use of his boot. And there were the penalties, always the penalties – just as in 2004, England lost to Portugal in a shoot-out.

It is hard to judge Eriksson's England tenure objectively. On paper, the results were good: Eriksson was both England's longest-serving manager since Sir Alf Ramsey and the only one other than him to take England to three major tournament quarter-finals. But England would have traded in two of those for a final appearance, or even the win that the nation craved.

And Eriksson had arguably the best England squad since 1970. In Rio Ferdinand, John Terry, Gary Neville and Ashley Cole we had the best defence in world football, and each of David Beckham, Frank Lampard and Steven Gerrard finished in the top three of the Ballon d'Or, the latter two during Eriksson's time in charge. Wayne Rooney was a generational talent. Given Eriksson's high salary and obvious calibre, his results were underwhelming.

But how much of that comparative disappointment was down to Eriksson and how much down to pure misfortune? His team was twice eliminated on penalties, the results of which were beyond anyone's control, but they came after 120-minute matches that England could have won. He also suffered galling injuries (pre- or mid-tournament) to Beckham, Gary Neville, Rooney and Gerrard.

However history judges Eriksson, the FA were again searching for another manager and, after the experiment with a foreign coach, it seemed obvious that they would look for one of their own. Steve McClaren had become the first English manager for eight years to win a major trophy in England and had taken Middlesbrough to seventh place in the Premier League, as well as the UEFA Cup Final. A new man was in the hot seat.

Right, from top: Frank Lampard walks back after missing his penalty against Portugal in the shoot-out of their quarter-final tie at the 2006 World Cup; Jamie Carragher has his penalty saved after being forced by the referee to retake it; England's players stand motionless after being eliminated from the tournament.

Opposite: Steven Gerrard looks dejected after England's second consecutive tournament exit on penalties, to Portugal and at the quarter-final stage.

PROFILE:
DAVID BECKHAM

It was a Baptist church on Nottingham's Mansfield Road that embodied the witch-hunt perfectly. "God forgives even David Beckham," blinked the neon yellow sign outside, referencing the events of June 30, 1998.

Three years later, Beckham was England's hero. His last-minute free-kick against Greece had not just saved the nation's hopes of automatic World Cup qualification, but completed one of the most pronounced comebacks in the history of English football.

The hateful reaction to Beckham's sending-off against Argentina in 1998 was indicative not just of England's desperation for tournament success, but also the mistrust of Brand Beckham. By 1998, he was a player with ideas above his station – at least in the eyes of half the nation. The pop star girlfriend, constantly changing haircut and fashion decisions (Jean Paul Gaultier sarong and all) clashed with England's expectation of a sporting superstar.

It was hardly Beckham's fault that he was young, good-looking and successful, but the green-eyed monster still grumbled and groaned. England's World Cup exit caused mourning, but Beckham's own demise prompted cackles and hoots of derision. This was not merely a sporting mistake, but a cultural comeuppance.

Beckham's emphatic rebounding from his lowest ebb was not his greatest feat – that lay in the manner of his absolution. For Beckham did not simply fall back into line, achieving acceptance through conformity; he pulled English football forward to meet him. Beckham was not English football's first superstar, but he did usher in a new age of footballer as global celebrity. English football would not have been left behind without him, but Beckham increased the sport's profile in every continent of the world.

Yet Beckham was not principally a cultural behemoth but an ambassador for English football. He embraced the trappings of fame without losing sight of the game, so managing to simultaneously act as a sex icon, fashion icon and sporting icon. In doing so, Beckham changed the rose-tinted and archaic view of our sporting champions, which had

Opposite: David Beckham celebrates his free-kick equaliser against Greece that secured England's place at the 2002 World Cup and completed his redemption arc.

Above: Beckham lines up to make his England debut against Moldova in September 1996.

Below: Beckham is shown a red card for kicking out at Diego Simeone during England's last-16 tie against Argentina at the 1998 World Cup.

progressed from stiff upper lip gentility to rough-and-ready muscularity, updating it appropriately for a modern, multicultural Britain.

Part of Beckham's iconic status is to be found in the humility that keeps him grounded – and therefore liked. Beckham seems comfortable with fame but only through learned behaviour, accepting it without ever revelling in the limelight. It is highly unusual for someone so ubiquitous to be so popular. Beckham is adored and admired by many, but disliked by very few. It is equally rare for anyone under the age of 50 to be afforded the status of national treasure; Beckham did so with 15 years to spare.

"David Beckham is Britain's finest striker of a football not because of God-given talent but because he practises with a relentless application that the vast majority of less gifted players wouldn't

contemplate," Sir Alex Ferguson once said, and therein lies the secret to the success of his Class of 92. Gary Neville, Phil Neville, Nicky Butt and Beckham were all very good footballers who maximised their ability through determination and hunger.

Never was this more true than in the case of Beckham, who studied free-kicks and crosses in the aftermath of World Cup 98 so fastidiously that he became like a monk on a journey to enlightenment. Beckham would speak years later about his obsessive-compulsive tendencies, but this was a means to staying strong amid adversity. It transformed him into the best crosser and free-kick taker in the game, and one of the best of all time on both counts.

Throughout his career, Beckham's commitment to practice was legendary, less a deliberate tactic than a natural instinct. "I remember being 13 and seeing my mum looking after three kids and then still working until 11 p.m. cutting hair," Beckham said in an interview with the *Daily Telegraph* in 2015. "My dad used to go out at 6 a.m. and come back at night covered in oil stains from working in the kitchens. They instilled that hard work ethic into me, and I want to do the same for my children."

The defining moment in Beckham's career came not in 1998 or 2001, but in November 2000 when he was made England captain for the first time under Peter Taylor, a decision ratified by Sven-Göran Eriksson. After battling to alter his post-Diego Simeone reputation, Beckham thrived when handed responsibility. The following season was his best in Manchester United colours, but the armband gave Beckham an increased clarity in his role as leader through example. From St Etienne onwards, his career had been a fight not to let anyone down; captaincy was the recognition of that fight.

But we cannot end anywhere but Old Trafford, at 4.57 p.m. on October 6, 2001. The greatest thing about Beckham's free-kicks were

that he, the goalkeeper, defensive wall and everyone watching knew what he was trying to do, yet they were impossible to stop. They were a battle, not between Beckham and the opposition, but between Beckham and the ball. If he placed it in the corner of the goal with the trajectory and pace that he practised for hours on end, nothing else mattered.

On that Saturday afternoon, with England's hopes fading, Beckham left the mortal football world and entered the ethereal. There were people watching hundreds of miles away who were shaking uncontrollably at the enormity of the situation, unable to control their emotions. The technique demonstrated by England's captain was remarkable, but the calmness under intense pressure was unfathomable. For a generation, it remains the greatest single moment of football fandom, when a nation rejoiced and anointed its king.

"I just want people to see me as a hard-working footballer, someone that's passionate about the game, someone that – every time I stepped on the pitch – I've given everything that I have, because that's how I feel," Beckham said after retiring. "That's how I look back on it and hope people will see me." How could they see anything else?

In that quote lies Beckham's true appeal. He was a prototype for a new breed of footballer, but one with an old-fashioned outlook on life. He had all the trappings of fame, but none of the airs or graces that many celebrities use to wilfully separate themselves from the hoi polloi. Beckham was a leader of English football, but only through example. In all the right ways, he was a, and perhaps even *the* – sportsman of our times.

Opposite above: Beckham is presented with the captain's armband for the first time by caretaker England manager Peter Taylor.

Opposite below: Beckham celebrates scoring a penalty – England's winner – in their group game against Argentina at the 2002 World Cup.

Above: Beckham jumps to the sky after scoring his free-kick against Greece in 2001. The game was played at Old Trafford (spot the Manchester United shirts in the crowd).

Below: Beckham waves to the crowd after England beat Belarus in October 2009. It was his final cap for his country.

CHAPTER FOURTEEN

UNFULFILLED
POTENTIAL

2006–2016

THE OPENING OF ENGLAND'S NEW NATIONAL STADIUM ALWAYS HAD THE POTENTIAL TO SUFFER DELAYS. THE ORIGINAL DATE OF 2003 WAS PUSHED BACK, FIRST TO 2005 AND THEN 2006, BEFORE BEING OFFICIALLY OPENED ON MAY 17, 2007 FOR THE FA CUP FINAL. AFTER SEVERAL YEARS OF TOURING THE COUNTRY, GIVING SUPPORTERS THE CHANCE TO WATCH ENGLAND PLAY IN DIFFERENT CITIES, THE TEAM HOSTED A FRIENDLY AGAINST BRAZIL AT WEMBLEY ON JUNE 1, 2007.

The new stadium was an extraordinary feat of engineering, mirroring the endeavour of its predecessor. With a capacity of 90,000 for live football and with 166 executive suites, Wembley was a modern stadium for a new age that aimed to retain the history and emotion of the old theatre. It would become the fourth-highest capacity stadium primarily used for football in the world. The iconic twin towers were replaced by an arch 134 metres (440 feet) high, which allowed the stadium to be seen from across the capital.

By the time England called Wembley home again, Steve McClaren had already been in position for 10 months and was experiencing the same issues as his predecessor. England's World Cup 2006 squad had contained four players aged 30 or above, and three of them – David Beckham, Sol Campbell and David James – were dropped for McClaren's first squad. John Terry was made permanent captain.

McClaren's England did beat Andorra and Greece in its first two competitive matches, scoring nine goals in the process. But between October 2006 and March 2007, England went five games without a victory, a run that included three qualifiers against Macedonia, Croatia and Israel in which England failed to score a goal. Their place at Euro 2008 was in doubt, despite two automatic qualification places in their group.

England and McClaren did respond, winning five consecutive matches by the same 3–0 scoreline. But when England lost 2–1 in Russia, despite leading with only a quarter of the game remaining, it piled the pressure upon a final group game at Wembley against Croatia. It was clear what England had to do: win handsomely and they would top the group; win less handsomely or draw and they would finish second, thanks to a better head-to-head record against Russia; lose, and they would face the ignominy of third place.

It was a miserable night at Wembley. As the rain teemed down, England were attacked repeatedly by a rampant Croatia team and went 2–0 down within 15 minutes. England finally pushed forward after half-time thanks to the leadership and drive of substitute Beckham,

controversially dropped from the starting XI. But having saved themselves once, England succumbed to a Mladen Petric winner and had no response. Not only would England miss the European Championship for the first time since 1984, it was to signal the end of another England manager.

For the second time in three appointments, there was no serious domestic option. The highest-placed English manager to complete the previous Premier League season was Steve Coppell, whose promoted Reading team finished eighth and were then relegated the season after.

Fabio Capello had always been the FA's number one choice and was reportedly the only coach interviewed for the position. Although Capello had no experience of international management, there was no doubting his record. The Italian had won league titles in each of the three previous seasons, with Juventus (later revoked after a financial scandal) and Real Madrid. Capello's disciplinarian approach was heralded as a positive move after the more laissez-faire strategy of his two predecessors.

Capello enjoyed an extended honeymoon during his first 18 months in charge. England won their first three matches of World Cup 2010 qualifying 5–1, 4–1 and 3–1, representing their best-ever start to a qualification campaign. That included a 4–1 win over Croatia in Zagreb that acted as revenge for the dismal defeat of November 2007, with Theo Walcott scoring the first competitive England hat-trick in seven years. England won 12 of their first 15 matches under Capello, the exceptions being friendly defeats away to Spain and France and a draw with the Czech Republic. The friendly highlight was a 2–1 win in Berlin, central defenders Terry and Matthew Upson scoring the goals.

England qualified with supreme ease for World Cup 2010. Their only defeat came against Ukraine in a dead rubber away fixture after top place in the group had already been assured. England scored 34 goals in 10 games and conceded only six. They beat top seeds Croatia by an aggregate scoreline of 9–2, fully exacting their revenge. Rooney was the star, with eight goals in the last seven group games suggesting that he was among the best forwards in world football. When England

Opposite: Steve McClaren stands underneath an umbrella as he watches England lose to Croatia in November 2007. It would be his last game in charge.

Below: Croatia's players celebrate their first goal at Wembley in November 2007. Defeat would mean England failed to qualify for Euro 2008.

won all three pre-tournament friendlies against Egypt, Mexico and Japan, there was little sign of what would follow in South Africa.

The World Cup was a humbling experience for England. Their cause was not helped by Terry being stripped of the captaincy and his replacement Rio Ferdinand being injured in a training session before the tournament and forced to pull out. But England were handed a favourable group-stage draw that they wasted by drawing against the USA and Algeria. Their attacking bluntness – just two goals in three group games – meant that they fell into second place.

That half of the draw was extraordinarily strong and contained Germany, Argentina, Spain and Portugal rather than the potentially less troublesome route of Ghana and Uruguay to reach the semi-finals. It mattered not. In Bloemfontein, England were outclassed by Germany from start to finish, soundly beaten 4–1. Even if the match officials had spotted that Frank Lampard's equaliser had crossed the line (a clanging error that prompted the introduction of goal-line technology), England would not have won.

Why had England fallen so far behind? The 2010 World Cup was a tournament during which the major nations had abandoned their previous

stereotypes in the successful search for something new. The Netherlands became an aggressive, physically imposing team that was the antithesis of the Johan Cruyff model. Germany entertained with free-flowing, counter-attacking football. Spain took their lead from Barcelona, winning the World Cup with an emphatic commitment to possession football.

And England had changed too, but not to good effect. The attacking impetus and pressing of qualifying had given way to lethargic, safety-first football that their opponents found easy to defend against. It was as if England had been smothered by the fear of failure rather than taking the chance to seize the progress that lay within their grasp. England's potential route to the semi-finals – the USA, Algeria, Slovenia, Ghana and Uruguay – was surely their least demanding in major tournament history. And yet they were suffocated by their own flaws.

Capello came in for stinging criticism. The discipline that had been welcomed at the start of his tenure was now a stick with which to beat him – the accusation was that England's players had been shouted at till they retreated into their shells.

There was also a suspicion that England's players lacked the flexibility of their peers. Spain often played without a recognised striker. Thomas Müller was impossible to tie down into one position.

Lionel Messi roamed across the forward line, sprinkling magic wherever he made contact with the ball. England had a more rigid system and were found wanting because of it.

English domestic football was on a high at the time. The Premier League had boasted six Champions League finalists in five years between 2005 and 2009 and those teams included a plethora of England internationals: Gerrard, Lampard, Michael Carrick, Owen Hargreaves, Ferdinand, Rooney, Jamie Carragher, Joe Cole, Ashley Cole, Terry, Sol Campbell and Paul Scholes. But that failed to translate cohesively into the international arena.

Opposite above: John Terry and Matthew Upson celebrate after Upson has scored England's opening goal in a 2–1 friendly win over Germany in Berlin in November 2008.

Opposite below: England's players celebrate John Terry's winner in the friendly victory over Germany. The win marked a run of five consecutive victories in three months during Fabio Capello's early reign.

Above: Wayne Rooney is congratulated by Fabio Capello after England's 5–1 home victory over Croatia during their qualifying campaign for the 2010 World Cup.

> " "HODGSON INHERITED A TEAM THAT HAD QUALIFIED FOR THE EUROS WITH EASE, A PROCESS THAT WAS BECOMING A VERY POSITIVE ENGLAND TEAM HABIT." "

The most obvious issue was that of pathways. England's squad at the 2010 World Cup was not only the oldest at the tournament but had the highest average age of any England World Cup squad in history – 16 of the 23 players were aged 28 or over. But who was pushing through? Twenty-one-year-old Theo Walcott was one controversial omission, but between 2008 and the World Cup, Capello had only given a debut to one player under the age of 22. That was Joe Hart, who travelled to South Africa.

Only 85 of the 220 players who started on the opening weekend of the 2010–11 Premier League season were English; that total dropped even further until rebounding in August 2019 to 83 players. The rise of billionaire ownership and rampant commercialisation of the Premier League had led to increased transfer budgets and made England's top flight the highest-spending division in world football. But deeper pockets meant a greater ability to attract the best foreign players in the world at the expense of potential domestic talent.

Capello signed a new contract to stay on until after Euro 2012, but he eventually left before the tournament after a dispute with the FA and took the Russia job. Roy Hodgson, considered as a potential candidate when Capello was appointed, now succeeded him.

Hodgson inherited a team that had qualified for the Euros with ease, a process that was becoming a very positive England team habit. They were unbeaten in their eight matches, topping the group by six points despite drawing home and away against Montenegro. England's best performances came away from Wembley, beating Switzerland and Wales 3–1 and 2–0 respectively.

Hodgson had little preparation time before Euro 2012, but he publicly committed to reducing the average age of the squad. England topped their group having beaten Sweden and Ukraine and drawn against France but were eventually defeated on penalties by Italy – the usual method of heartbreak. Hodgson and his side could have few complaints,

Opposite above: Frank Lampard's shot against Germany in the last 16 of the 2010 World Cup beats Manuel Neuer and clearly crosses the line, but no goal is given.

Opposite below: Lampard cannot hide his disbelief that the goal is not awarded. It would have brought England level at 2–2 – they eventually lost 4–1.

Below: Thomas Müller scores Germany's third goal past David James, to extinguish England's hopes of World Cup progression.

Above: Roy Hodgson, Wayne Rooney (left), Andy Carroll (centre) and Steven Gerrard (right) enjoy a joke as England prepare to train in Donetsk's Donbass Arena during Euro 2012.

Below: Scott Parker celebrates after England beat Ukraine in their Euro 2012 group stage match (left), Andy Carroll celebrates after scoring England's opener in their 3–2 victory over Sweden in the group stage. It is England's first ever competitive victory against the Swedes (right).

Opposite: Joe Hart (left) and Glen Johnson (right) embrace after the final whistle of England's win over Ukraine. The 1–0 victory means England top their group ahead of France.

however, as they were outclassed by an Italian side that controlled the tempo of the quarter-final. Five Italians attempted more than 75 passes in 120 minutes. No England player managed more than 45.

England reverted to type for World Cup 2014 qualifying. They were again unbeaten, this time finishing above a resurgent Ukraine team. But the tournament only brought more emphatic proof of England's declining fortunes on the biggest stage. Hodgson persevered with youth (the tournament was actually labelled as England looking to the future rather than obsessing about their short-term prospects in Brazil), with more than a quarter of the squad aged 23 or under. But England were eliminated after two matches, before drawing their final game 0–0 against Costa Rica. England had scored just five goals in their previous eight World Cup finals matches.

If England's youthful squad in 2014 suggested that they were gearing up towards a stronger showing at Euro 2016, there was little evidence. Sloppy draws against Russia and Slovakia meant that England finished behind Wales in their group, but a last-16 draw against Iceland offered optimism for further progression. Instead, England fell to their lowest major tournament ebb since the humiliation against the USA in 1950. After Wayne Rooney's early penalty, England succumbed to defeat against a team representing a nation of only 330,000 people. Hodgson had no choice but to leave his position.

And so England were left deeply perplexed. If the arguments over player pathways, youth development, coaching systems and an overload of foreign players in the domestic league all carried some weight, they did not fully explain the major tournament underperformance. Between 1996 and 2016, 12 different European nations reached the semi-finals of either the World Cup or European Championship: France, Croatia, the Netherlands, Turkey, Germany, Italy, Portugal, Spain, the Czech Republic, Greece, Russia and Wales. England lagged behind some names on that list, but certainly not all.

Perhaps this was a question of pressure. England had produced some of their best major tournament performances – in 1986 and 1990 – when there were lower pre-tournament expectations; the same was arguably also true in Euro 96, coming immediately after the failure to qualify for the 1994 World Cup. They had been repeatedly ruthless in qualifying only to fail to beat teams of a similar standard at the main event. Did this suggest something that went beyond the technical ability of the players and coaches and reflected something in the national psyche, some kind of inability to rise to the occasion or choke under pressure? And, if so, who could hope to solve it?

Opposite: Raheem Sterling takes on Iceland's Jón Daði Böðvarsson during their last-16 tie at Euro 2016.

Above: Kolbeinn Sigþórsson celebrates putting Iceland 2–1 up. Sigþórsson's goal would be the winner, eliminating England to represent the team's lowest major tournament ebb since the 1950 World Cup.

Following pages: England's players express their disappointment after Iceland's equaliser, coming shortly after Wayne Rooney had given England the lead.

PROFILE:
WAYNE ROONEY

We have become predisposed not to pile undue pressure on young players with superstar potential. History is littered with young players who have been compared to the greats of yesteryear: the new Maradona, the new Duncan Edwards, the new Ronaldo. In some cases it can inspire and in others it can suffocate, creating unfair expectations that these protégés struggle to live up to.

But in 2004, on the eve of England's European Championship quarter-final with Portugal, Sven-Göran Eriksson was confident enough to hail England's new star as the future. "I don't remember anyone making such an impact since Pelé in the 1958 World Cup," said Eriksson. "Rooney is absolutely fantastic, not only at scoring goals but the way he plays football – he's a complete footballer."

The following evening, Rooney suffered a broken metatarsal 27 minutes into the match. England were 1–0 up at the time. They would eventually lose on penalties, hampered by Rooney's departure and furious about a late disallowed Sol Campbell winner.

Three months later, Rooney made his Manchester United and Champions League debut on the same September evening at Old Trafford. He was the most expensive teenager in the world, running on to the pitch in front of 70,000 expectant supporters and with his new manager calling him "the best young player this country has seen in 30 years". Pressure? What pressure? Rooney scored a hat-trick against Fenerbahce.

It's easy to forget in hindsight just how young Rooney was. Before he had turned 19, he had led England at Euro 2004, the second-highest scorer in the competition despite playing only 258 minutes. He had taken the domestic club scene by storm, scoring his first Premier League goal at the age of 16 to inflict Arsenal's first league defeat in 30 matches. He had moved to Manchester United and, as already noted, scored three times on his debut to become England's youngest goalscorer in the Champions League.

The majesty of Rooney lay in his instincts. When looking back on that first United hat-trick he said how the game passed by in a blur. "Afterwards, we went back with my wife and two friends and I just sat down and couldn't believe what had just happened. That was when it really hit me that I'd just scored a hat-trick on my debut."

That indicates Rooney's natural propensity to perform. Preferring to roam deep and wide to be heavily involved in play, his prowess at finding pockets of space, and knowing when and how to shoot, was fantastic. Watching him in an England shirt, particularly during his formative years, was to witness a player who was simultaneously learning on the job but also remarkably fully formed. That is a thing of great wonder.

But what made Rooney extra special was that the innate skill was blended with a "street footballer" persona that was distinctly South American in feel. It was not that Rooney did not have immense skill – that was never in doubt. But he combined that with a hunger and steel for scoring goals and winning games that was always evident in his England performances. "When you score the goal it's like you come up for air and you can hear the crowd, the atmosphere, for that four or five seconds," he once said. That feeling of overwhelming joy propelled him on.

Coupled to that was Rooney's vision, colloquially referred to as the "football brain". Early in his career, he would compare football to snooker or chess, constantly requiring thought about what might happen three or four passes later in the move. That is a marker of every great footballer, but particularly those who cannot rely upon extraordinary pace. You beat your opponent in the mind and then punish them with your feet.

Opposite: Wayne Rooney celebrates scoring England's second goal against Switzerland in their Euro 2016 qualifying match. It was Rooney's 50th goal for his country, breaking Bobby Charlton's goalscoring record.

Above: Rooney scores his second goal against Croatia during a group stage match at Euro 2004.

"I DON'T REMEMBER ANYONE MAKING SUCH AN
IMPACT SINCE PELÉ IN THE 1958 WORLD CUP."

SVEN-GÖRAN ERIKSSON ON WAYNE ROONEY'S IMPACT AT THE 2004 EUROPEAN CHAMPIONSHIP

Rooney became a proud exponent of visualisation techniques. A few days before a match, he would ask those responsible which kit the team would be wearing in a few days. Using that information, he would sit or lie down, close his eyes and run through potential scenarios in which he was given space to shoot. By playing out those moments before the game, he believed it prepared him better to react positively in the forthcoming match. His record is proof that it worked.

There is no argument that Rooney peaked at a younger age than most, partly due to his accelerated maturity and partly because he played an astonishing amount of football in his early years as a professional. By the end of 2006–07, when still just 21, Rooney had amassed 213 club appearances and had played 38 times for England. When he scored against Iceland at Euro 2016, he could not have imagined it would be his last international goal. England were ahead, favourites for the match and Rooney was just 30.

And there were regrets. England were not able to perform as Rooney would have liked during his three World Cup campaigns, although he did score against Uruguay in 2014. More than half of Rooney's major tournament goals came at the age of 18 in 2004.

But then those laments were easily outweighed by the contributions Rooney made as an England player, captain and goalscorer. He ended his international career as his country's record goalscorer and record appearance-maker for an outfield player. Thirty-seven of his 53 goals came in competitive matches and he scored more than once on 10 different occasions. Harry Kane may eventually break Rooney's goalscoring record, but only Raheem Sterling in the current squad has more than half his number of caps.

And one thing remained constant until the last minute of Rooney's last cap: he was desperate to succeed. Not through the selfish demand for records or honours or even plaudits, but because he grew up wanting to play for England – and spent his entire career just as determined to make England the best they could be.

Above: Rooney scored England's opener against Switzerland at Euro 2004. It was his first major tournament goal.

Opposite: Rooney watches on as England beat Trinidad & Tobago at the 2006 World Cup (top left); Rooney is honoured on the occasion of his final cap, against the USA in November 2018 (top right); Rooney celebrates scoring England's opener against Ukraine in their Euro 2012 group stage match (bottom).

CHAPTER FIFTEEN

HOPE SPRINGS ETERNAL

1990 – 2013

TED COPELAND DID NOT LEAVE HIS POSITION AS ENGLAND WOMEN'S MANAGER PURELY BECAUSE OF THE TEAM'S FAILURE TO QUALIFY FOR THE 1999 WORLD CUP – DOING WELL IN A GROUP CONTAINING GERMANY AND NORWAY WAS ALWAYS GOING TO BE A HUGE TASK. BUT WITH THE FA EYEING A FULL-TIME APPOINTMENT AND COPELAND ALREADY FIVE YEARS IN HIS ROLE, IT WAS DECIDED THAT MEANINGFUL CHANGE WAS REQUIRED.

H ope Powell had not expected to be offered the job. When a call came from the FA, Powell had been considering retiring to take up youth coaching and assumed she was being offered a role in that area. But Powell had underestimated her suitability. She held a UEFA 'B' Licence, knew the England set-up inside out, had never been shy about sharing her thoughts on improving the coaching system, and was familiar with the players at her disposal. She was also offered the chance to oversee the game from grassroots to elite level.

Powell threw herself into her new position with remarkable vigour. She organised a national talent identification camp, assembling players from the 50 women's football academies nationwide on the recommendations of the coaches within them. She reorganised the piecemeal, often volunteer-run coaching systems into a more formal structure. She overhauled the scouting system, forming a group of 20 talent identification scouts who would trawl the country in search of new talent. She worked with Umbro to design specialised kits for her players for the first time; each kit would have the right fit and cut for each squad member. She also asked the FA to recompense players for time taken off work, allowing the senior squad to meet up four days before matches.

But Powell's biggest concern was over the fitness of her players when compared to the best teams in the world – Germany, the USA

Above: Chelsea host Bristol Academy in the Women's Super League. The league's first season began in April 2011, but moved to a winter league format for the 2017/18 season.

Opposite: Gillian Coultard crouches, disappointed, after England lose 1–0 at home to Germany in March 1998.

and Sweden. England had developed a bad habit of conceding late goals (including in Powell's first match, a 1–0 defeat to Sweden) and England's new manager believed that there was a pronounced drop-off in performance in the last half hour of their games.

After appointing two full-time physios, an exercise scientist and a chief medical officer, Powell got funding for several regional conditioning centres. They provided England players with the chance to carry out extra training and conditioning with specialised coaches on top of their club training. With Sweden and Germany's players training between eight and 10 times per week and England's part-time players often only training twice a week at club level, Powell witnessed a rapid improvement in physical fitness.

On the pitch, Powell favoured a switch to a 4-3-3 formation that she believed better allowed for the full-backs to push forward, the midfield to be creative and the skilful wide players to drift inside to support a central striker. Under Copeland, England had tended to play direct football but with improved fitness the team could now press without the ball and use short, sharp passes with it.

Powell's first task as coach of the national side was to lift England out of its relative ignominy. Finishing bottom of their World Cup qualifying group meant that a two-legged play-off against Romania would determine whether England fell to 'B' status, which would make future World Cup qualification impossible. A dominant 6–2 aggregate victory allayed any immediate fears.

Qualification for the 2001 European Championship was a slightly easier proposition after the misery of 1999. England were again drawn against Norway, but Portugal and Switzerland were ranked lower than England and second place would lead to a play-off for one of the remaining tournament spots. Powell showed her intent by peppering her squads with young players – Kelly Smith, Rachel Yankey, Rachel Brown and Katie Chapman would become fixtures in the team over the next decade. Having beaten Ukraine away 2–1 in Borispol in the first leg, England won the return fixture 2–0 at Leyton Orient's Brisbane Road, in front of a crowd of over 7,000, a record for an England home international.

England then headed to Germany with realistic expectations. Having been drawn in an incredibly hard group that also included Sweden and Russia, England drew their first game 1–1 against the Russians, but were comfortably beaten by both Germany and Sweden to finish bottom.

Although Powell had expected such results, she believed that her players had been overawed by the quality of opposition in their final two matches; England were still playing catch-up. Her response was to form a number of England age-level teams (Under-21, Under-19, Under-17 and, eventually, Under-15). Friendlies at each level would give players more big-game experience. The Under-21, Under-19 and Under-17 teams would all be coached in the same 4-3-3 system as the senior team, allowing a smooth transition as players matured.

Just as important to Powell and the FA was the education system. As recently as 2002, the percentage of girls within schools who had access

to football was lower than 15 per cent. Many of those without that access could potentially enjoy football as a healthy pursuit and some of them might have an untapped talent for the sport. The FA began to work with schools, offering support for coaching within PE lessons, and after-school facilities. The mission was not just to identify talent, as with the boys, but to allow and empower girls to play football and so, over time, create an environment in which a generation of female players were enthused to participate and see football as a potential career option. The road would be long, but foundations had at least been laid.

Qualification for World Cups had always been a tough ask for England. They competed at only one of the first three editions (1991, '95 and '99) and again missed out under Powell in 2003. With only five places from Europe up for grabs (and Sweden, Norway and Germany virtual certainties to be involved), England finished second in their qualification group behind a German side that won all their games, scoring 30 goals and conceding just one. England won their play-off semi-final against Iceland but were beaten 1–0 home and away by a strong France team in the final. The FA made it clear that Powell's position was not only based on tournament qualification, but the frustration of having to wait another four years for the World Cup to come around again was clear to see.

That pervading sense of missed opportunity was wrapped tightly around England for the European Championship in 2005. Powell had been a key proponent of the successful bid to bring the tournament to England, but the team was again placed in a group with a powerhouse

(Sweden), as well as two other northern European countries (Denmark and Finland) who had made great strides. England beat Finland 3–2 in their opening match, but lost to Denmark, having dominated the match for long periods and conceding twice in the last ten minutes. Needing a draw against Sweden to progress, England conceded early and were unable to get the equaliser required.

Off the field, the 2005 European Championship was a huge success. England's opening game at the City of Manchester Stadium attracted 29,029 spectators, the highest ever for an official England match and the biggest ever for a European Championship game. England's matches were watched by eight million people on the BBC. Powell knew that England had competed in each of their three matches, but was acutely aware that major tournament progress was required to accelerate interest.

Faith and hope were to be found in the personnel within Powell's Euro 2005 squad. Of the 20 players selected for the tournament, 15 were aged 25 or under and more than a third of the squad were under 23. Seventeen-year-old Karen Carney had become an overnight sensation with her injury-time winner against Finland; Alex Scott, Fara Williams

Opposite: Hope Powell battles with Germany's Steffi Jones during England's World Cup qualifying defeat to Germany in March 1998.

Above: A group of excited young England fans pose for a photo before England's game against Finland at the City of Manchester Stadium, part of the 2005 UEFA Women's Euro, which England hosted.

and Eni Aluko were all still eligible for Under-21 football; Casey Stoney was 23; two of the senior squad members, Kelly Smith and Faye White, were still only 26 and 27 respectively. Four of those players would end up in the top five of England's record appearance makers.

Success started to come at the World Cup in 2007. England qualified for the first time in five attempts, finally topping a qualification group ahead of France and the Netherlands and remaining unbeaten in their eight matches. At the tournament itself, England produced brilliant performances to draw with Japan (another late goal conceded) and Germany – England were the only team in the tournament to stop eventual champions Germany from scoring. A comprehensive quarter-final defeat to the USA disappointed Powell, but only in accordance with her own high standards.

Further good news for Powell and England came in March 2009 with the introduction of central contracts for 20 of England's most regular players. This was intended to help players focus on training – particularly their fitness – around their full-time jobs, meaning they were restricted to 24 hours of other employment a week. The remuneration of £16,000 may have been a drop in the ocean compared to the riches of the men's game, but Powell welcomed the move heartily.

And proof of sustainable improvement came in the summer of 2009. The expansion of the women's Euros from eight to 12 teams gave England an easier passage, remaining unbeaten in a group that contained Spain and the Czech Republic as their closest competitors. Powell's side

Opposite: Faye White and Alex Scott (No. 2) celebrate after England secure a 0–0 draw with Germany in Shanghai at the 2007 Women's World Cup.

Below: England line up for their team photo before their Euro 2009 group match against Russia in Helsinki in August 2009. England would win the game 3–2.

 "THE MISSION WAS NOT JUST TO IDENTIFY TALENT, AS WITH THE BOYS, BUT TO ALLOW AND EMPOWER GIRLS TO PLAY FOOTBALL AND SO, OVER TIME, CREATE AN ENVIRONMENT IN WHICH A GENERATION OF FEMALE PLAYERS WERE ENTHUSED TO PARTICIPATE AND SEE FOOTBALL AS A POTENTIAL CAREER OPTION."

suffered wobbles – a 0–0 draw at home to the Czechs, going in 1–0 down at half-time against the same opponent in the return fixture, going 2–0 down to Spain when needing only a draw to qualify – but England stepped up in the knockout stages of the tournament proper.

Having drawn with Sweden and surprisingly lost to Italy in the group stage, England beat Finland in the quarter-finals and the Netherlands in a tense semi-final settled by Jill Scott's extra-time winner in Tampere. That took them to a maiden official major tournament final against Germany for which England were clear outsiders. Despite twice responding to trail 3–2 with 60 minutes played, Germany's class eventually told and England were beaten 6–2. Powell declared herself proud of the journey, but she insisted that Germany's level had to be the target for the FA and England.

If England's men's team at major tournaments became defined by agonising penalty shoot-out defeats, the 2011 World Cup brought the women under the same umbrella. With no automatic qualification for the tournament, England won their group with an almost perfect record (their only dropped points were away in Spain) and then beat Switzerland home and away in the play-off despite Rachel Brown's harsh sending-off midway through the second leg.

It was a tournament of surprises. Canada were ranked sixth in the world but finished dead last, losing all three games in a fierce group that also contained Germany, France and Nigeria. Norway were knocked out of the group stage by emerging nation Australia. Japan caused the biggest shock of all, beating Germany on penalties in the quarter-finals and winning the tournament – also on penalties – against the USA.

That provided much regret for England, who had beaten Japan 2–0 in their group but lost on penalties to France after an 88th-minute equaliser from Élise Bussaglia. In consecutive World Cups, England had been the only team to draw with the champions and then the only team to beat them.

Back at home, just before the World Cup, the inaugural season of the Women's Super League began. Originally intended to begin in 2010, it was a summer league until 2016 when it switched to follow the typical English football calendar. Eight clubs competed in the first season, with Arsenal crowned champions. Clubs were permitted to pay players a maximum of £20,000 per year, later increased to £26,000, allowing for increased professionalism that was intended to support the development of international-standard players.

By 2013, it became clear that freshness was needed. England had qualified for the European Championship in now typically breezy fashion (Powell didn't lose a qualifying match in her last 10 years in charge) but, after England travelled to Sweden with high expectations, the tournament was a bitter disappointment. They lost their opening match 3–2 to Spain (Alexia Putellas' winner was highly controversial) and drew against Russia, meaning that a victory against France was needed to make the quarter-finals. The French were irresistible in a 3–0 win that sent England home, bottom of their group. It was their worst European Championship performance since 2001.

Left: Jill Scott is congratulated by her teammates after scoring the winner in England's Euro 2009 semi-final match against the Netherlands at the Tampere Stadium in Finland.

Powell admitted in her autobiography that the relentlessness of the job had drained her of energy. The 2011 World Cup was followed by the 2012 Olympics, then European Championship qualifying, the tournament and World Cup 2015 qualifying. England's manager also expressed concern about the players' ability to cope with the intense media pressure that grew with the increased coverage received by the team. Ultimately, Powell paid the price. At a meeting at Wembley on August 8, 2013, she was informed that the FA were terminating her contract and seeking a successor. Eight days later, the news was made public.

To some extent, Powell became a victim of her own success. Although her job was not initially judged on results, England's performances between 2007 and 2011 (two World Cup quarter-finals and a European Championship final) created expectations that they were unable to match in 2013. In some ways, Powell's eventual sacking is a compliment to her: she demanded the higher standards that were ultimately used to judge her. She was also responsible for far more than the 11 players on the pitch, helping to establish and then overseeing the pathways that would create a better future for those who followed her.

Opposite: Faye White misses a crucial penalty during the shoot-out against France in the quarter-final of the Women's World Cup in 2011 (above), some of England's players struggle to watch the penalties (below).

Above: White is consoled by Anita Asante (left) and Steph Houghton (right) after England are knocked out by France.

Right: Hope Powell shouts some instructions to her players during England's Euro 2013 group game against Russia. England would draw 1–1.

HOPE POWELL

This is not a competition. There is no definitive ranking of a sport's trailblazers and nor should there be. They stand on each other's shoulders, giants who are able to see broader horizons, a better view, thanks to the giants who came before them. Those who take the game forward typically do not do it for recognition or plaudits.

So let's simply say that Hope Powell runs like a seam through the re-rise of women's football in England. In every year between 1983 and 2013, she either played for, or managed, the England national team. In 2002, Powell was awarded an OBE. In 2010, a CBE followed for her services to the women's game. Even then, Powell appreciated the personal honour but was keen to place it in a more helpful context: "It's even better for the women's game to be honoured and this award is great recognition for all the hard work and efforts of the staff and players that I work with."

Growing up in Greenwich, south-east London, Powell would play in the concrete cages on Harriott Close. At first the boys would refuse to pick her because she was a girl. When one day she was finally selected, they wished they hadn't.

As a child, Powell became briefly famous for breaking down walls. At the age of 11, she played for her Abbey Wood School against another local comprehensive. After the game, the opposition – who, coincidentally, had just been beaten – complained to the FA about the presence of a girl in the team and Powell and teammate Jane Bartley were banned. The story made the local newspapers and Powell's PE teacher unsuccessfully took up the cause.

Three years later, the school wrote to the Equal Opportunities Commission to appeal the ban and again failed. Powell was playing for her county but barred from inter-school football. In 2011, the age at which mixed football was permitted was increased from 11 to 13, but Powell continued to insist that it should be raised further. Boys and girls can play together until 17 in Germany and 19 in the Netherlands, while there are no restrictions in Norway and Sweden.

But Powell's talent was always likely to shine through and she was forever ahead of the curve. At the age of 12 she signed official terms with Millwall Lionesses and joined the first-team squad a year later. By the age of 16 she had made her senior England debut against the Republic of Ireland. At 19 she passed her first coaching qualifications and worked within Crystal Palace's community programmes alongside playing.

Powell went on to enjoy a fruitful international career, scoring 35 goals in 66 appearances over 16 years. But it was as a coach and manager that she truly thrived, pushing back the boundaries of coaching excellence in the women's game. In 2003, Powell became the first woman to earn UEFA's Pro Licence, the highest qualification in the

Opposite: Powell takes England training in 2003. She became the first full-time manager of the England women's team in 1998.

Below left: Powell taking part in the warm-up before an England Under-18 friendly against Finland in March 1999.

Below right: Powell watches on during the Euro 2009 final as England play Germany in Helsinki on September 10, 2009. England would lose the game 6–2.

game. When she retired from England playing duty in 1998 to become the team's manager, Powell achieved the triple milestones of becoming the England women's team's first full-time coach, the youngest-ever manager of an England side and the first non-white appointment.

The Pro Licence was a big deal for Powell and for women's football in England. As Powell herself said, there was no tokenism at play here: you were either a good enough coach to pass the course or you weren't. Twenty-six years after being banned from playing with the boys at school, Powell had risen to the top of her profession through study and assessment alongside them.

As part of her role, Powell was not content to merely organise the senior national team. She understood the importance of player development and pathways, particularly in an industry striving for improvement and international recognition. She became responsible for overseeing, if not coaching, the entire England youth set-up from Under-15s to Under-21s, as well as a player development scheme and coach mentoring scheme.

Powell's England were not always successful on the pitch. They did not qualify for the World Cup in 1999 or 2003 and won one group stage game at the 2001 and 2005 Euros combined. But her career was framed not just by England's tournament record, but by the growth of the sport in this country. In 2012, a year before she left her post, the Olympic final at Wembley was watched by 80,000 spectators. If England did go on to reach the semi-finals of three major tournaments following her departure (2015, 2017 and 2019), the importance of the foundations laid by Powell cannot be overstated.

The breadth and pressure of Powell's responsibilities within the England set-up could have drowned many. But she flourished in her roles as coach, role model, campaigner and ambassador for the elite and grassroots game. Powell was instrumental in persuading the FA to agree to a central contract system that would allow players to focus their time on football rather than full-time jobs. That contract system, more than anything else, facilitated the improvement of standards. She was not just unafraid to ruffle feathers; she delighted in it.

Powell has received many honours. As a standard-bearer for the women's game, she became the natural figurehead of her sport. Alongside the CBE and OBE, she has received honorary degrees from seven English universities: Roehampton, Nottingham, Loughborough, Leeds, St Mark and St John, York and East London.

She treats them all the same. "These honours were not just for me, but for women's football," Powell wrote in her autobiography. "It was a real measure of what progress was being made in the game. We were being recognised. We were visible… The honours have come to me. But so far as I'm concerned, they are for the game."

Opposite: Powell gives a speech during the Women's Leadership Programme Graduation at The Institute of Directors in London in March 2017.

Above: Powell receives her CBE medal in November 2010 at Buckingham Palace. She was rewarded for her services to the growth of women's football.

CHAPTER SIXTEEN

A BRIGHT FUTURE

2016–PRESENT

ALL ERIC DIER HAD TO DO WAS SCORE A PENALTY. ONE KICK, DIRECTED INTO A PLACE WHERE COLOMBIA GOALKEEPER DAVID OSPINA COULD NOT EXTEND HIS DIVE OR STRETCH HIS GLOVE. ONE KICK THAT WOULD OFFER ENGLAND SOLACE AFTER SO MANY PENALTY SHOOT-OUT HEARTBREAKS. A QUARTER-FINAL PLACE WAS ON THE LINE, BUT NOBODY – WHETHER THEY WERE STANDING ON THE HALFWAY LINE AS DIER STRODE FORWARD OR WATCHING AT HOME DARING TO DREAM – COULD ESCAPE THE BIGGER PICTURE: ENGLAND WERE SEEKING SALVATION.

BBC Sport's montage of that shoot-out details the mental journey every England supporter embarked upon during those five angst-ridden minutes. Each penalty is interspersed with memories of penalty dejection that has littered the country's recent history – 1990, 1996, 1998, 2004, 2006, 2012. When Dier's penalty, aimed perfectly into the bottom left-hand corner of Ospina's goal, rippled the net, the montage reaches its crescendo and innumerable different celebrations combine to provoke an outpouring of football's most beautiful emotions: joy, relief, exhilaration and glorious disbelief.

England did not win the World Cup in 2018. They were beaten by Croatia in a semi-final, proof that agony always has the upper hand in the end. But that wholly fails to explain the lasting legacy of that tournament in this country. England and Gareth Southgate had engineered levels of hope that the team had not generated in at least 12 years. For the first time in far too long, England's players seemed to grow into the tournament and embraced the pressures that inevitably came with it. From the ignominy of Iceland in 2016, England had altered expectations and evaporated the negative stereotypes. We had something to believe in again.

And that, after all, is what international football, all football, is about. Managers and players will always be judged by results, and nobody is

Above: A 2–1 Euro 2020 semi-final victory over Denmark in July 2021 sparks delirious celebrations from the England players and staff.

Opposite: Gareth Southgate watches on with a smile during England's Euro 2020 training camp.

Opposite above: Jordan Pickford celebrates after saving Carlos Bacca's penalty during the 2018 World Cup last-16 shoot-out against Colombia.

Opposite below: England's players rush from the halfway line after Eric Dier's penalty gives England their first ever World Cup shoot-out win.

Above: England's players rush to congratulate goalkeeper Pickford, the new hero of the hour.

campaigning for an alternative attitude there. But for supporters, the true joy of football lies not in what happens but how it makes you feel. At the 2018 World Cup, supporting England was a four-week-long journey of redemption that justified all the pain that had preceded it.

Euro 2020, delayed for a year because of COVID-19, took that journey forward and further improved the sense of national unity. The team became the first side since the heroes of 1966 to reach a major tournament final, kept five successive clean sheets and only trailed for eight minutes in the entire tournament. They finally beat Germany in a tournament match, romped through a quarter-final and, with the youngest England tournament squad in 63 years, grew into the competition. They recreated the atmosphere of 2018 so people could party in their own homes, gardens, pubs and town squares. Wembley hosted six of England's games and witnessed joyous scenes after the quarter- and semi-finals.

But there was to be no moment of triumphal salvation that the country craved. That relentless clock, ticking on past the 55-year mark of England's hurt, has not yet been stopped. But England are a team

Above: Raheem Sterling celebrates opening the scoring against Germany. England's 2–0 victory was the first competitive win against the Germans in almost two decades.

Right: John Stones outjumps Thomas Müller of Germany at Euro 2020, on the way to helping England to a fourth consecutive clean sheet.

Opposite: Harry Kane wheels away and is mobbed by his teammates after scoring the goal that sends England to the final of Euro 2020.

moving in the right direction, the only side to reach the semi-finals of both the 2018 World Cup and the 2020 European Championships. The wounds of yet another agonising penalty shoot-out defeat shouldn't overshadow these landmark performances.

Whether England's continued improvement is sustainable in part depends on the development of its young talent. The construction and opening of St George's Park in 2012 was one step to ensure it. The National Football Centre has 12 training pitches including an exact replica of Wembley's playing surface and is the training base for all men's and women's England teams. It has state-of-the-art facilities relating to conditioning, coaching, medical support and sports science.

But success goes beyond mere facilities. In 2014, two years after the National Football Centre opened, the FA launched "England DNA" with the intention of creating a world-class environment to produce young male and female players and a smooth pathway for them to develop as international footballers. It focused on five key aims: who we are, how we play, the future England player, how we coach and how we support.

In 2017, England's men's team witnessed the first direct results of the St George's Park and England DNA model. The country's youth sides enjoyed an unprecedented year of success, winning the Under-20 World Cup, the Under-19 European Championship, the Under-17 World Cup and reaching the final of the Under-17 European Championship. More encouraging even than England's performance in 2017 is the development of numerous players who played a part. Of the squads that competed in those tournaments, 11 have gone on to play for the senior side: Phil Foden, Callum Hudson-Odoi, Reece James, Jadon Sancho, Mason Mount, Fikayo Tomori, Dean Henderson, Lewis Cook, Ainsley Maitland-Niles, Dominic Solanke and Dominic Calvert-Lewin.

What's more, many of these players have established themselves as key components in their clubs' success. They share winners' medals in the Premier League, Champions League and Europa League and most were regular starters in the most recent Premier League, Bundesliga and Serie A seasons. The willingness to move abroad, either on loan or permanent deals, offers England a roundedness that previous eras have lacked. These players are the future.

And they have stepped up not just as footballers, but people whom we can be immensely proud to call our own. Marcus Rashford has worked very visibly to help ease the problem of child poverty. Jordan Henderson is an ambassador not just for Liverpool and England but of the NHS, becoming the NHS Charities Together champion. Raheem Sterling has spoken out about systemic and overt racism. Other England players joined together to campaign against online hate and social media abuse. It is not always easy being a footballer in 2021 – your wealth inevitably draws criticism and can coerce you into the status of a role model. But this generation of players have the opportunity to make a difference and have the maturity and eloquence to seize it.

Opposite: Gareth Southgate consoles Bukayo Saka after England's penalty defeat to Italy in the final of Euro 2020. The England manager is no stranger to penalty heartbreak, but knows better than most that it can inspire great things to come.

Below: Luke Shaw becomes the first male England player to score a tournament final goal since Geoff Hurst in 1966, as England take the lead against Italy at Wembley.

If England's men's teams have improved across the board over the last half decade, the improvement – at least in terms of their major tournament performance – of the senior England women's team has been even more pronounced: three consecutive major tournament semi-finals, all achieved on foreign soil. At the 2015 World Cup, England finished third to become the most successful senior England World Cup squad of either gender since 1966.

It was a brilliant tournament for England and new coach Mark Sampson. After losing 1–0 to France in their opening fixture, they beat both Mexico and Colombia 2–1 despite injury-time consolation goals. In the knockout stages, England rose to the occasion by repeating the 2–1 trick against previous champions Norway and hosts Canada. The disappointment of a semi-final defeat to Japan, Laura Bassett's last-minute own goal sinking the game, was followed by victory over Germany in the third-place play-off in Edmonton. It was the first time that England had ever beaten Germany. Hope Powell's insistence that the Germans should be England's watermark had been realised.

And England kicked on from 2015, albeit after a disappointing SheBelieves Cup in 2016, when they lost to Germany and the USA, and drew with France. They qualified with ease for Euro 2017, scored 10 goals in their three group-stage matches and then produced a landmark performance in the quarter-finals, ending a 42-year, 19-match winless run against France. The Netherlands were simply too strong for Sampson's side in the semi-finals, but this was real progress.

At the 2019 World Cup, with Phil Neville replacing Sampson, England reached their third consecutive major tournament semi-final, a feat the men's team have never achieved to date. The group stage saw England edge past Argentina, Scotland and Japan without ever really punishing their opponents. That changed in the knockout stages, where England beat both Cameroon and Norway 3–0 in

Below: The England squad celebrate in the changing room after a 3–0 victory over Japan makes them winners of the SheBelieves Cup in March 2019.

Opposite: Ellen White leaps in celebration after scoring England's second goal during the 2019 Women's World Cup last-16 match against Cameroon in Valenciennes, France.

similar circumstances, with Ellen White scoring a second goal just before half-time in each game to put the Lionesses firmly in control.

A semi-final against heavy favourites (and eventual champions) the USA always promised to be tough for England, but there were lingering regrets that the outcome was not different. White had a goal ruled out by a marginal VAR offside decision, Steph Houghton missed a penalty to give England an equaliser with five minutes remaining, and two minutes after that Millie Bright was sent off for a second yellow card.

More than England's consistency at World Cups and European Championships, it was the development of a wonderful crop of world-class players that offered the most persuasive cause for congratulation. Karen Bardsley, Lucy Bronze and Houghton were all selected in the all-star squad after the 2015 World Cup. Bronze and Houghton retained their places after Euro 2017 and were joined by Golden Boot winner Jodie Taylor. Bronze was named as the runner-up in both the World Cup Golden Ball and the Ballon d'Or Feminin in 2019, while Ellen White was the joint-top scorer at the World Cup that year.

And English domestic women's football has seen an overdue rise to European prominence. The investment of time and money in Chelsea and Manchester City's women's teams has challenged Arsenal's domestic dominance. In 2021, Chelsea became the first English team in 14 years to reach the UEFA Women's Champions League final. Emma Hayes is heralded as one of the best coaches in the game. Fran Kirby and Bronze are still regarded among the top 15 players in the world and the WSL has begun to attract the very best: Alex Morgan, Christen Press, Sam Mewis, Sam Kerr, Vivianne Miedema and Pernille Harder all competed in 2021.

As ever with the women's game, focus must also shift to participation and interest. In July 2019, it was confirmed by the BBC that 47 per cent of the UK population watched the coverage of the Women's World Cup semi-final against the USA. The TV audience of 11.7 million was the highest for a live broadcast in that year to date. The Lionesses are making waves and the country is enthusiastic to witness their progress under Sarina Wiegman, their first non-British head coach.

The grassroots game continues to expand. In 2017, the Football Association launched its Gameplan for Growth programme, an initiative that aimed to double the number of women and girls playing regular football within the space of three years, which would ultimately ensure that England continues to compete on the world stage at every age level. In May 2020, that target was realised with 3.4 million participants and an increase of 54 per cent in the number of women's and girls' teams, to 9,251.

And the elite women's game will have its own National Football Centre. In 2019, plans were confirmed for the construction of a major training and leisure facility in West Cheshire. It will act as an elite performance centre for women's and girls' football, and will be the first facility of its kind in Europe.

Above: England's new manager Sarina Wiegman. Wiegman succeeded Phil Neville as permanent coach in September 2021.

Opposite: England's stars of tomorrow: Ellie Roebuck (top left), Jadon Sancho (top right), Mason Mount (bottom left) and Georgia Stanway (bottom right).

COVID-19 created the biggest crisis in English football's post-war history. Not since World War II had there been a longer break between league fixtures. Football could never hope to sit apart from the spread of a global pandemic and so inevitably, like everything else, became subservient to it. COVID-19 has raised serious questions about the sustainability and financial health of the English football pyramid and the game, in this country and across the world, faced an uncertain future.

England's national teams were also affected by football's pause. Euro 2020 was postponed by a year and with a reduced number of supporters at the majority of matches. The inter-country travel that UEFA saw as a key reason to have a continent-wide tournament was not possible. The Women's European Championship, due to be hosted by England – the country's first exclusive major tournament since 2005 and second since 1996 – was also postponed by 12 months to July 2022.

If football without supporters was better than no football at all, it remained a bleak version of its normal self. Players and managers spoke extensively about missing match-going fans, not because they wanted to offer vague media-friendly platitudes but because they genuinely deeply missed them. Going to a match is, for many millions of people in this country, a pursuit born partly out of habit, partly out of loyalty and partly out of wonder at the way football makes them feel. For everyone who was accustomed to sport forming an integral part of their lives, its absence was catastrophic.

At times, international football can feel like it is eclipsed by the mania and money of the club game and its transfer market frenzy. Lovers of the game know different. The England teams, their rises and their falls, their glorious successes and their agonising failures and everything in between, are football at its best. For all the undisputed brilliance of club football, nothing unites people like the international game.

And the appetite for enjoying and enduring the fortunes of our national teams shows no sign of diminishing. No TV audience is ever as big, and no national mood is ever dictated by the kick of a ball or the miss of a chance as much as when England are playing at a major tournament. Whatever else happens and however painful the exit, there will always be another one around the corner and always more history waiting to be written.

Left: England supporters wave flags to support the national team during a Euro 2020 qualifier against Bulgaria in September 2019.

APPENDIX

LEGACY NUMBERS

ENGLAND CAP HOLDERS
1872–2021

MEN'S SENIOR TEAM

1–100

1 Robert Barker
2 Harwood Greenhalgh
3 Reginald Welch
4 Frederick Chappell
5 John Maynard
6 John Brockbank
7 Charlie Clegg
8 Arnold Smith
9 Cuthbert Ottaway
10 Charles Chenery
11 Charles Morice
12 Alec Morten
13 Leonard Howell
14 Alfred G Goodwyn
15 Pelham von Dunop
16 Alexander Bonsor
17 William Clegg
18 Rev. Walpole Vidal
19 Hubert Heron
20 William Kenyon-Slayney
21 Robert Ogilvie
22 Alfred Stratford
23 Francis Birley
24 John Owen
25 Charles Wollaston
26 Hawley Edwards
27 Robert Kingsford
28 William Carr
29 Edward Haygarth
30 William Rawson
31 Charlie Alcock
32 Herbert Rawson
33 Richard Geaves
34 Arthur Savage
35 Edgar Field
36 Frederick T Green
37 Beaumont Jarrett
38 Ernest Bambridge
39 Walter Buchanan
40 Charles Smith
41 Frank Heron
42 Arthur Cursham
43 Monty Betts
44 William Lindsay
45 Lindsay Bury
46 Alf Lyttleton
47 Billy Mosforth
48 John Bain
49 Cecil Winfield Stratford
50 Conrad Warner
51 Jack Hunter
52 Edward Lyttelton
53 Norman Bailey
54 Percy Fairclough
55 John Wylie
56 Henry Wace
57 Rupert Anderson
58 Claud Wilson
59 Edward Parry
60 Heathcote Sorby
61 Herbert Whitfield
62 Reginald Birkett
63 Edward Christian
64 Harold Morse
65 James Prinsep
66 Arnold Hills
67 Arthur Goodyer
68 Francis Sparks
69 Charlie Bambridge
70 Albemarle Swepstone
71 William Brindle
72 Ted Luntley
73 Segar Bastard
74 Sam Widdowson
75 John Sands
76 Fred Hargreaves
77 Tom Marshall
78 Harry Cursham
79 Clem Mitchell
80 Edward Johnson
81 John Hawtrey
82 Alf Harvey
83 Arthur Bambridge
84 Tot Rostron
85 Jimmy Brown
86 George Tait
87 Jack Hargreaves
88 George Holden
89 Reg Macauley
90 John Rawlinson
91 Alf Dobson
92 Doctor Greenwood
93 Canon Robert King
94 Horace Barnet
95 Arthur Brown
96 Howard Vaughton
97 Alf Jones
98 Percival Parr
99 Percy de Paravicini
100 Bruce Russell

101–200

101 Stuart Macrae
102 Harry Goodhart
103 Harry Moore
104 Jack Hudson
105 Oliver Whateley
106 Rev. Frank Pawson
107 Arthur Dunn
108 Nevill Cobbold, MA
109 Billy Rose
110 Joe Beverley
111 Charles Wilson
112 William Bromley Davenport
113 Billy Gunn
114 James Forrest
115 Herby Arthur
116 Arthur Walters
117 Percy Walters
118 Joe Lofthouse
119 Ben Splisbury
120 Jimmy Ward
121 Kenny Davenport
122 John Dixon
123 Rev. Andrew Amos
124 Tom Danks
125 Dick Baugh
126 George Shutt
127 Ralph Squire
128 Charley Dobson
129 Teddy Leighton
130 Fred Dewhurst
131 Tinsley Lindley
132 Thelwell Pike
133 George Brann
134 Bob Howarth
135 Charlie Mason
136 George Haworth
137 Teddy Brayshaw
138 Jimmy Sayer
139 Bob Roberts
140 Billy Moon
141 Harry Allen
142 Frank Saunders
143 Cecil Holden-White
144 George Woodhall
145 John Goodall
146 Dennis Hodgetts
147 Albert Aldridge
148 Bob Holmes
149 Charlie Shelton
150 Billy Bassett
151 Albert Allen
152 Albert Fletcher
153 Arthur Lowder
154 Billy Betts
155 Jack Southworth
156 Bill Townley
157 Bill Rowley
158 Tommy Clare
159 Charles Wreford-Brown
160 David Weir
161 Alf Shelton
162 Frank Burton
163 Jack Brodie
164 Harry Daft
165 Jack Yates
166 Henry Hammond
167 Johnny Holt
168 Edmund S Currey
169 Harry Wood
170 Jack Barton
171 Charlie Perry
172 Fred Geary
173 Nat Walton
174 Joe Marsden
175 Alf Underwood
176 Jem Bayliss
177 George Cotterill
178 Arthur Henfrey
179 Leonard Wilkinson
180 Tom Porteous
181 Elphinstone Jackson
182 Albert Smith
183 Alf Milward
184 Edgar Chadwick
185 George Toone
186 Harry Lilley
187 Anthony Hossack
188 Norman Winckworth
189 George Kinsey
190 Cunliffe Gosling
191 Joe Schofield
192 Rupert Sandilands
193 Jack Cox
194 Mick Whitham
195 Charlie Athersmith
196 Jackie Pearson
197 John 'Jack' Devey
198 Jack Reynolds
199 Chris Charsley
200 Hugh Harrison

201–300

201 Fred Pelley
202 Norman C Cooper
203 Robert Topham
204 Gilbert Oswald Smith
205 Rev. Walter Gilliat
206 John Sutcliffe
207 James Turner
208 Jimmy Whitehead
209 Fred Spiksley
210 Leslie Gay
211 Joe Reader
212 Jimmy Crabtree
213 Harry Chippendale
214 Vaughan Lodge
215 Arthur Topham
216 John Veitch
217 Ernest Needham
218 Rab Howell
219 Tom Crawshaw
220 Steve Bloomer
221 Frank Becton
222 Rev. George Raikes
223 Bill Oakley
224 Richard Barker
225 Hugh Stanbrough
226 Gerard Dewhurst
227 Steve Smith
228 Cuthbert James Burnup
229 John William Robinson
230 Bill Williams
231 Bernard Middleditch
232 Fred Wheldon
233 Harry Bradshaw
234 Willy 'Billy' Foulkes
235 Howard Spencer
236 Frank Forman
237 Tommy Morren
238 Charlie Richards
239 Ben Garfield
240 Tom Perry
241 Tom Booth
242 Jack Hillman
243 Phil Bach
244 Jimmy Settle
245 Fred Forman
246 Harry Thickitt
247 Harry Johnson
248 Arthur Turner
249 Dan Cunliffe
250 Charles Sagar

301–400

401–500

251 Fred Priest
252 Arthur Chadwick
253 Reginald 'Tip' Foster
254 Dr. Geoffrey Wilson
255 Alf Spouncer
256 John Plant
257 Charles B Fry
258 William Jones
259 George Hedley
260 Herbert Banks
261 Jack Cox
262 Matt Kingsley
263 Albert Wilkes
264 Billy Bannister
265 Walter Bennett
266 Billy Beats
267 Bertie Corbett
268 James Iremonger
269 Fred Blackburn
270 Bill George
271 Bob Crompton
272 Walter Abbott
273 Billy Hogg
274 Bert Lipsham
275 Jack Calvey
276 George Molyneux
277 Kelly Houlker
278 Tom Badderley
279 Tom Holford
280 Harry Hadley
281 Harry Davis
282 Jack Sharp
283 Vivian Woodward
284 Arthur Lockett
285 William Garraty
286 Joe Bache
287 Rex Reginald Corbett
288 Percy Humphreys
289 Arthur Capes
290 Herbert Burgess
291 Bert Lee
292 Herod Ruddlesdin
293 Billy Brawn
294 Alf Common
295 Arthur Brown
296 George Davis
297 Alexander Leake
298 Sam Wolstenholme
299 Bernard Wilkinson
300 Jock Rutherford

301 Stanley Harris
302 Tim Williamson
303 Billy Balmer
304 Jack Carr
305 Charlie Roberts
306 Dickie Bond
307 Frank Booth
308 Harry Linacre
309 Herbert Smith
310 Harold Hardman
311 Arthur Bridgett
312 Jimmy Ashcroft
313 Ben Warren
314 Colin Veitch
315 Sammy Day
316 Albert/Bert Gosnall
317 Ted Wright
318 Harry Makepeace
319 Albert Shepherd
320 Jimmy Conlin
321 Sam Hardy
322 Billy Wedlock
323 Bob Hawkes
324 John/Tim Coleman
325 George Hillsdon
326 Jesse Pennington
327 Irvine Thornley
328 Jimmy Stewart
329 George Wall
330 Harry Maskrey
331 Evelyn Lintott
332 Jimmy Windridge
333 Horace Bailey
334 Watty Corbett
335 Frank Bradshaw
336 Joe Cottle
337 Arthur Berry
338 Fred Pentland
339 Bert Freeman
340 George Holley
341 Harold Fleming
342 George Richards
343 Harold Halse
344 Bert Morley
345 Arthur Cowell
346 Andy Ducat
347 Billy Bradshaw
348 Bert Hall
349 Jack Parkinson
350 Billy Hibbert

351 Wally Hardinge
352 Albert Sturgess
353 Jock Simpson
354 George Woodger
355 Robert Evans
356 Kenneth Hunt
357 George Webb
358 Tom Brittleton
359 Jackie Mordue
360 Frank Jefferis
361 Bob Benson
362 Frank Cuggy
363 Tommy Boyle
364 George Utley
365 Charles Buchan
366 George Elliott
367 Joe Smith
368 Ernie Scattergood
369 Hugh Moffat
370 Joe McCall
371 Charlie Wallace
372 Harry Hampton
373 Eddie Latheron
374 Joe Hodkinson
375 Billy Watson
376 Frank Buckley
377 Danny Shea
378 Harry Martin
379 Horace Colclough
380 Bobby McNeal
381 Eddie Mosscrop
382 Fanny Walden
383 Joe Smith
384 Arthur Knight
385 Jimmy Bagshaw
386 Sidney Bowser
387 Bobby Turnbull
388 Jackie Carr
389 Jack Cock
390 Tommy Clay
391 Frank Barson
392 Arthur Grimsdell
393 Sam Chedgzoy
394 Alf Quantrill
395 Ephraim Longworth
396 Bob Kelly
397 Fred Morris
398 Jack Mew
399 Dickie Downs
400 Fred Bullock

401 Billy Walker
402 Bert Coleman
403 Warney Cresswell
404 Jack Silcock
405 Jack Bamber
406 George Wilson
407 Tom Bromilow
408 Harry Chambers
409 Harold Gough
410 Tommy Smart
411 Bert Smith
412 Bert Bliss
413 Jimmy Dimmock
414 Howard Baker
415 Jack Fort
416 Albert Read
417 Percy Barton
418 Archie Rawlings
419 Jimmy Seed
420 George Harrison
421 Jerry Dawson
422 Tommy Lucas
423 Frank Moss
424 Billy Kirton
425 Ernie Simms
426 Teddy Davison
427 Fred Titmuss
428 Max Woosnam
429 Bill Rawlings
430 Billy Smith
431 Sam Wadsworth
432 Dicky York
433 Edward Taylor
434 Jack Harrow
435 David Mercer
436 Frank Osborne
437 Owen Williams
438 Tommy Magee
439 Vic Watson
440 Fred Kean
441 Norman Bullock
442 Jackie Hegan
443 Jack Tresadern
444 Fred Tunstall
445 John Alderson
446 Harry Jones
447 Seth Plum
448 Jimmy Seddon
449 Norman Creek
450 Frank Hartley

451 Ernie Williamson
452 Bill Ashurst
453 Basil Patchitt
454 George Thornewell
455 Jimmy Moore
456 Harry Bedford
457 Tommy Urwin
458 Billy Moore
459 Harold Miller
460 Alfred Bower
461 Harold Pantling
462 Tommy Meehan
463 Joe Bradford
464 Ted Hufton
465 Bill Brown
466 Tommy Roberts
467 Graham Doggart
468 Ron Sewell
469 Tommy Mort
470 David Jack
471 Clem Stephenson
472 Charlie Spencer
473 Billy Butler
474 Freddie Ewer
475 George Blackburn
476 Stanley Earle
477 Vivian Gibbins
478 Harry Storer
479 James 'Fred' Mitchell
480 Harry Healless
481 Harry Hardy
482 Jack Butler
483 Frank Roberts
484 Arthur Dorrell
485 Dick Pym
486 Jack Hill
487 Len Graham
488 Tommy Cook
489 Jack Townrow
490 Frederick Fox
491 Tom Parker
492 Billy Felton
493 Billy Bryant
494 George Green
495 Frank Hudspeth
496 George Armitage
497 Sam Austin
498 Syd Puddefoot
499 Claude Ashton
500 Willis Edwards

501–600

501 Roy Goodall
502 Ted Harper
503 Jimmy Ruffell
504 George Ashmore
505 Dick Hill
506 Sam Cowan
507 Joe Spence
508 Joe Carter
509 Tosh Johnson
510 Albert McInroy
511 George Brown
512 Jack Brown
513 George Waterfield
514 Willie Pease
515 William Ralph Dean
516 Louis Page
517 Herbert Jones
518 Sid Bishop
519 Joe Hulme
520 Arthur Rigby
521 Tom Cooper
522 Harry Nuttall
523 Jack Ball
524 Dan Tremelling
525 Reg Osborne
526 Alf Baker
527 Tom Wilson
528 Ben Olney
529 Ernie Blenkinsop
530 Vincent Matthews
531 Jack Bruton
532 George Stephenson
533 Len Barry
534 Jack Hacking
535 Jim Barrett
536 Austen Campbell
537 Ernie Hyne
538 Ernie Hart
539 Russell Wainscoat
540 Joe Peacock
541 Hugh Adcock
542 Edgar Kail
543 George Camsell
544 Len Oliver
545 Albert Barrett
546 Eric Brook
547 Harry Hibbs
548 Billy Marsden
549 Alf Strange
550 Maurice Webster
551 Sammy Crooks
552 Ellis Rimmer
553 Tony Leach
554 Gordon Hodgson
555 Jimmy Hampson
556 Harry Burgess

557 Eric Houghton
558 Herbie Roberts
559 Jackie Crawford
560 Hugh Turner
561 Tommy Graham
562 Joe Tate
563 Tom 'Pongo' Waring
564 Harry Roberts
565 Jack Smith
566 Charlie Gee
567 Cliff Bastin
568 Harold Pearson
569 George Shaw
570 Peter O'Dowd
571 Sam Weaver
572 Bobby Barclay
573 Arthur Cunliffe
574 Lewis Stoker
575 Alf Young
576 Teddy Sandford
577 Eric Keen
578 Ron Starling
579 George Hunt
580 John Pickering
581 Johnny Arnold
582 Eddie Hapgood
583 Tom White
584 Wilf Copping
585 Albert Geldard
586 Jimmy Richardson
587 Billy Furness
588 Jim Allen
589 Tommy Grosvenor
590 Jack Bowers
591 David Fairhurst
592 Arthur Rowe
593 Willie Hall
594 Frank Moss
595 Raich Carter
596 Horace Burrows
597 Fred Tilson
598 Tom Gardner
599 Joe Beresford
600 Cliff Britton

601–700

601 Jack Barker
602 Jackie Bray
603 Stanley Matthews
604 Ray Bowden
605 Ray Westwood
606 George Male
607 Ted Drake
608 Jackie Bestall
609 Walter Alsford

610 Bob Gurney
611 Fred Worrall
612 George Eastham
613 Bill Richardson
614 Wally Boyes
615 Ted Sagar
616 Septimus Smith
617 Ralph Birkitt
618 Jack Crayston
619 Dickie Spence
620 Harold Hobbis
621 Bernard Joy
622 Sam Barkas
623 Jimmy 'Nat' Cunliffe
624 Harry Holdcroft
625 Bert Sproston
626 Ted Catlin
627 Tom Smalley
628 Billy Scott
629 Freddie Steele
630 Joe Johnson
631 George Tweedy
632 Vic Woodley
633 Alf Kircham
634 Tom Galley
635 Len Goulden
636 Ken Willingham
637 Harry Betmead
638 Jackie Robinson
639 Joe Payne
640 Stan Cullis
641 George Mills
642 Jack Morton
643 Micky Fenton
644 Eric Stephenson
645 Don Welsh
646 Frank Broome
647 Tommy Lawton
648 Doug Wright
649 Ronnie Dix
650 Reg Smith
651 Bill Morris
652 Joe Mercer
653 Pat Beasley
654 Leslie Smith
655 Frank Swift
656 Laurie Scott
657 George Hardwick
658 Billy Wright
659 Neil Franklin
660 Henry Cockburn
661 Tom Finney
662 Wilf Mannion
663 Bobby Langton
664 Harry Johnston
665 Jimmy Mullen

666 Eddie Lowe
667 Stan Mortensen
668 Tim Ward
669 Phil Taylor
670 Stan Pearson
671 Jack Howe
672 Johnny Aston
673 Jimmy Hagan
674 Len Shackleton
675 Jackie Milburn
676 Ted Ditchburn
677 Alf Ramsey
678 Jack Rowley
679 Jack Haines
680 Johnny Hancocks
681 Eddie Shimwell
682 Roy Bentley
683 Bill Ellerington
684 Jimmy Dickinson
685 Johnny Morris
686 Bert Williams
687 Bert Mozley
688 Peter Harris
689 Jesse Pye
690 Bernard Streten
691 Willie Watson
692 Jack Froggatt
693 Bill Jones
694 Laurie Hughes
695 Bill Eckersley
696 Eddie Bailey
697 Allenby Chilton
698 Jackie Lee
699 Lionel Smith
700 Leslie Compton

701–800

701 Les Medley
702 Nat Lofthouse
703 Harold Hassall
704 Jim Taylor
705 Vic Metcalfe
706 Bill Nicholson
707 Arthur Willis
708 Mal Barrass
709 Tommy Thompson
710 Gil Merrick
711 Jackie Sewell
712 Len Phillips
713 Arthur Milton
714 Ivor Broadis
715 Tommy Garrett
716 Billy Elliott
717 Ronnie Allen
718 Redfern Froggatt

719 Tommy Taylor
720 Johnny Berry
721 Albert Quixall
722 Dennis Wilshaw
723 Derek Ufton
724 Stan Rickaby
725 Ernie Taylor
726 George Robb
727 Ron Staniforth
728 Roger Byrne
729 Harry Clarke
730 Johnny Nicholls
731 Syd Owen
732 Beddy Jezzard
733 Bill McGarry
734 Ray Wood
735 Bill Foulkes
736 Johnny Wheeler
737 Ray Barlow
738 Don Revie
739 Johnny Haynes
740 Brian Pilkington
741 Bill Slater
742 Frank Blunstone
743 Jimmy Meadows
744 Ken Armstrong
745 Duncan Edwards
746 Peter Sillett
747 Ron Flowers
748 Ron Baynham
749 Jeff Hall
750 Geoff Bradford
751 Ronnie Clayton
752 Bill Perry
753 John Atyeo
754 Reg Matthews
755 Colin Grainger
756 Gordon Astall
757 Johnny Brooks
758 Alan Hodgkinson
759 Derek Kevan
760 David Pegg
761 Eddie Hopkinson
762 Don Howe
763 Bryan Douglas
764 Alan A'Court
765 Bobby Robson
766 Jimmy Langley
767 Bobby Charlton
768 Colin McDonald
769 Tommy Banks
770 Eddie Clamp
771 Peter Brabrook
772 Peter Broadbent
773 Wilf McGuinness
774 Graham Shaw

775 Danny Clapton
776 Doug Holden
777 Warren Bradley
778 Jimmy Armfield
779 Norman Deeley
780 Jimmy Greaves
781 Tony Allen
782 Trevor Smith
783 John Connelly
784 Brian Clough
785 Eddie Holliday
786 Ron Springett
787 Ken Brown
788 Joe Baker
789 Ray Parry
790 Ray Wilson
791 Peter Swan
792 Dennis Viollet
793 Mick McNeil
794 Bobby Smith
795 Gerry Hitchens
796 John Angus
797 Brian Miller
798 Johnny Fantham
799 Ray Pointer
800 Johnny Byrne

801–900

801 Ray Crawford
802 Stan Anderson
803 Roger Hunt
804 Bobby Moore
805 Maurice Norman
806 Alan Peacock
807 Mike Hellawell
808 Chris Crowe
809 Ray Charnley
810 Alan Hinton
811 Brian Labone
812 Freddie Hill
813 Mike O'Grady
814 Bobby Tambling
815 Ron Henry
816 Gordon Banks
817 Gerry Byrne
818 Jimmy Melia
819 Gordon Milne
820 George Eastham
821 Ken Shellito
822 Terry Paine
823 Tony Kay
824 Bobby Thomson
825 George Cohen
826 Peter Thompson
827 Tony Waiters

828 Mike Bailey
829 Fred Pickering
830 Terry Venables
831 Gerry Young
832 Frank Wignall
833 Alan Mullery
834 Nobby Stiles
835 Jack Charlton
836 Barry Bridges
837 Alan Ball
838 Mick Jones
839 Derek Temple
840 Norman Hunter
841 Gordon Harris
842 Keith Newton
843 Geoff Hurst
844 Martin Peters
845 Ian Callaghan
846 Peter Bonetti
847 John Hollins
848 David Sadler
849 Cyril Knowles
850 Mike Summerbee
851 Alex Stepney
852 Colin Bell
853 Tommy Wright
854 Bob McNab
855 Gordon West
856 Francis Lee
857 Paul Reaney
858 John Radford
859 Terry Cooper
860 Jeff Astle
861 Emlyn Hughes
862 Ian Storey-Moore
863 Peter Osgood
864 Ralph Coates
865 Brian Kidd
866 Allan Clarke
867 Peter Shilton
868 Roy McFarland
869 Martin Chivers
870 Joe Royle
871 Colin Harvey
872 Peter Storey
873 Chris Lawler
874 Paul Madeley
875 Tommy Smith
876 Larry Lloyd
877 Tony Brown
878 Rodney Marsh
879 Malcolm Macdonald
880 Colin Todd
881 Tony Currie
882 Mick Mills
883 Frank Lampard

884 Jeff Blockley
885 Mick Channon
886 Ray Clemence
887 Kevin Keegan
888 David Nish
889 John Richards
890 Kevin Hector
891 Phil Parkes
892 Mike Pejic
893 Martin Dobson
894 Dave Watson
895 Stan Bowles
896 Trevor Brooking
897 Keith Weller
898 Frank Worthington
899 Alec Lindsay
900 Gerry Francis

901–1000

901 Dave Thomas
902 Steve Whitworth
903 Ian Gillard
904 Alan Hudson
905 Kevin Beattie
906 Dennis Tueart
907 Colin Viljoen
908 David Johnson
909 Brian Little
910 Trevor Cherry
911 Phil Neal
912 Phil Thompson
913 Mike Doyle
914 Phil Boyer
915 Ray Kennedy
916 Peter Taylor
917 Dave Clement
918 Tony Towers
919 Brian Greenhoff
920 Stuart Pearson
921 Jimmy Rimmer
922 Ray Wilkins
923 Gordon Hill
924 Joe Corrigan
925 Charlie George
926 Trevor Francis
927 John Gidman
928 Paul Mariner
929 Brian Talbot
930 Terry McDermott
931 Trevor Whymark
932 Steve Coppell
933 Bob Latchford
934 Peter Barnes
935 Tony Woodcock
936 Viv Anderson

937 Kenny Sansom
938 Laurie Cunningham
939 Kevin Reeves
940 Glenn Hoddle
941 Bryan Robson
942 Garry Birtles
943 Alan Devonshire
944 Russell Osman
945 Terry Butcher
946 Alan Sunderland
947 David Armstrong
948 Peter Ward
949 Eric Gates
950 Graham Rix
951 Alvin Martin
952 Peter Withe
953 Tony Morley
954 Steve Foster
955 Cyrille Regis
956 Paul Goddard
957 Steve Perryman
958 Ricky Hill
959 Gary Mabbutt
960 Luther Blissett
961 Sammy Lee
962 Mark Chamberlain
963 Derek Statham
964 Gordon Cowans
965 Graham Roberts
966 John Barnes
967 Danny Thomas
968 Steve Williams
969 Mark Barham
970 John Gregory
971 Paul Walsh
972 Nick Pickering
973 Nigel Spink
974 Mike Duxbury
975 Brian Stein
976 Alan Kennedy
977 Mark Wright
978 Terry Fenwick
979 Gary Lineker
980 Steve Hunt
981 Mark Hateley
982 David Watson
983 Clive Allen
984 Gary Stevens
985 Trevor Steven
986 Gary Bailey
987 Chris Waddle
988 Peter Davenport
989 Gary Stevens
990 Peter Reid
991 Kerry Dixon
992 Paul Bracewell

993 Chris Woods
994 Danny Wallace
995 Peter Beardsley
996 Steve Hodge
997 Tony Cottee
998 Tony Adams
999 Stuart Pearce
1000 Neil Webb

1001–1100

1001 Steve McMahon
1002 Mick Harford
1003 Gary Pallister
1004 David Rocastle
1005 Des Walker
1006 Paul Gascoigne
1007 David Seaman
1008 Mel Sterland
1009 Michael Thomas
1010 Alan Smith
1011 Brian Marwood
1012 Paul Parker
1013 Nigel Clough
1014 John Fashanu
1015 Steve Bull
1016 Dave Beasant
1017 Mike Phelan
1018 Nigel Winterburn
1019 David Platt
1020 Tony Dorigo
1021 Lee Dixon
1022 Ian Wright
1023 Lee Sharpe
1024 Dennis Wise
1025 Geoff Thomas
1026 David Batty
1027 David Hirst
1028 John Salako
1029 Earl Barrett
1030 Mark Walters
1031 Brian Deane
1032 Gary Charles
1033 Paul Stewart
1034 Paul Merson
1035 Andy Gray
1036 Andy Sinton
1037 Tony Daley
1038 Rob Jones
1039 Martin Keown
1040 Alan Shearer
1041 Carlton Palmer
1042 Keith Curle
1043 Nigel Martyn
1044 Paul Ince
1045 David White

1101–1200

1046 David Bardsley
1047 Les Ferdinand
1048 Teddy Sheringham
1049 Tim Flowers
1050 Stuart Ripley
1051 Graeme Le Saux
1052 Darren Anderton
1053 Matthew Le Tissier
1054 Kevin Richardson
1055 Steve Bould
1056 Barry Venison
1057 Rob Lee
1058 Steve Howey
1059 Neil Ruddock
1060 Steve McManaman
1061 Warren Barton
1062 Nick Barmby
1063 Andrew Cole
1064 Gary Neville
1065 John Scales
1066 David Unsworth
1067 Stan Collymore
1068 Colin Cooper
1069 Jamie Redknapp
1070 Steve Stone
1071 Gareth Southgate
1072 Robbie Fowler
1073 Jason Wilcox
1074 Sol Campbell
1075 Ian Walker
1076 Phil Neville
1077 Ugo Ehiogu
1078 David Beckham
1079 Andy Hinchcliffe
1080 David James
1081 Nicky Butt
1082 Paul Scholes
1083 Rio Ferdinand
1084 Chris Sutton
1085 Dion Dublin
1086 Michael Owen
1087 Lee Hendrie
1088 Tim Sherwood
1089 Ray Parlour
1090 Wes Brown
1091 Kevin Phillips
1092 Jamie Carragher
1093 Michael Gray
1094 Emile Heskey
1095 Jonathan Woodgate
1096 Kieron Dyer
1097 Frank Lampard
1098 Steve Guppy
1099 Steven Gerrard
1100 Gareth Barry

1101 Richard Wright
1102 Seth Johnson
1103 Chris Powell
1104 Michael Ball
1105 Gavin McCann
1106 Ashley Cole
1107 Joe Cole
1108 Michael Carrick
1109 Alan Smith
1110 Danny Mills
1111 Owen Hargreaves
1112 Trevor Sinclair
1113 Danny Murphy
1114 Wayne Bridge
1115 Michael Ricketts
1116 Darius Vassell
1117 Ledley King
1118 Lee Bowyer
1119 David Dunn
1120 James Beattie
1121 Paul Robinson
1122 Paul Konchesky
1123 Jermaine Jenas
1124 Francis Jeffers
1125 Wayne Rooney
1126 Matthew Upson
1127 John Terry
1128 Glen Johnson
1129 Scott Parker
1130 Alan Thompson
1131 Jermain Defoe
1132 Anthony Gardner
1133 Shaun Wright-Phillips
1134 Stewart Downing
1135 Andrew Johnson
1136 Kieran Richardson
1137 Zat Knight
1138 Luke Young
1139 Peter Crouch
1140 Rob Green
1141 Darren Bent
1142 Theo Walcott
1143 Aaron Lennon
1144 Chris Kirkland
1145 Micah Richards
1146 Ben Foster
1147 Joey Barton
1148 David Nugent
1149 Nicky Shorey
1150 David Bentley
1151 Joleon Lescott
1152 Scott Carson
1153 Ashley Young
1154 Dean Ashton
1155 Joe Hart

1156 Phil Jagielka
1157 Stephen Warnock
1158 Gabriel Agbonlahor
1159 Carlton Cole
1160 James Milner
1161 Tom Huddlestone
1162 Leighton Baines
1163 Adam Johnson
1164 Michael Dawson
1165 Kieran Gibbs
1166 Bobby Zamora
1167 Jack Wilshere
1168 Gary Cahill
1169 Kevin Davies
1170 Jordan Henderson
1171 Andy Carroll
1172 Jay Bothroyd
1173 Matt Jarvis
1174 Danny Welbeck
1175 Chris Smalling
1176 Phil Jones
1177 Jack Rodwell
1178 Kyle Walker
1179 Daniel Sturridge
1180 Fraizer Campbell
1181 Alex Oxlade-Chamberlain
1182 Martin Kelly
1183 Jack Butland
1184 Tom Cleverley
1185 John Ruddy
1186 Jake Livermore
1187 Ryan Bertrand
1188 Jonjo Shelvey
1189 Steven Caulker
1190 Raheem Sterling
1191 Leon Osman
1192 Ryan Shawcross
1193 Carl Jenkinson
1194 Wilfried Zaha
1195 Rickie Lambert
1196 Ross Barkley
1197 Andros Townsend
1198 Fraser Forster
1199 Adam Lallana
1200 Jay Rodriguez

1201–present

1201 Luke Shaw
1202 John Stones
1203 Jon Flanagan
1204 Fabian Delph
1205 Calum Chambers
1206 Nathaniel Clyne
1207 Harry Kane

1208 Ryan Mason
1209 Jamie Vardy
1210 Dele Alli
1211 Danny Ings
1212 Eric Dier
1213 Danny Rose
1214 Danny Drinkwater
1215 Marcus Rashford
1216 Tom Heaton
1217 Jesse Lingard
1218 Aaron Cresswell
1219 Michael Keane
1220 Nathan Redmond
1221 James Ward-Prowse
1222 Kieran Trippier
1223 Harry Maguire
1224 Harry Winks
1225 Jordan Pickford
1226 Ruben Loftus-Cheek
1227 Tammy Abraham
1228 Joe Gomez
1229 Jack Cork
1230 Dominic Solanke
1231 James Tarkowski
1232 Lewis Cook
1233 Trent Alexander-Arnold
1234 Nick Pope
1235 Ben Chilwell

1236 Jadon Sancho
1237 Nathaniel Chalobah
1238 Lewis Dunk
1239 Callum Wilson
1240 Alex McCarthy
1241 Declan Rice
1242 Callum Hudson-Odoi
1243 Mason Mount
1244 Tyrone Mings
1245 James Maddison
1246 Fikayo Tomori
1247 Phil Foden
1248 Mason Greenwood
1249 Conor Coady
1250 Kalvin Phillips
1251 Jack Grealish
1252 Ainsley Maitland-Niles
1253 Bukayo Saka
1254 Dominic Calvert-Lewin
1255 Reece James
1256 Harvey Barnes
1257 Dean Henderson
1258 Jude Bellingham
1259 Ollie Watkins
1260 Ben Godfrey
1261 Ben White
1262 Sam Johnstone

Opposite: Gareth Southgate poses with his commemorative England legacy cap. The caps and legacy numbers were introduced as part of the celebrations surrounding England men's 1,000th game in November 2019, all senior debutants now receive a cap with their unique legacy number embroidered on the front.

Above: England Lionesses are celebrating their landmark 50th anniversary in 2022, as well as hosting the UEFA Women's EURO 2022. There will be a very special unveiling of the complete legacy list of players that have appeared for England in this unique anniversary year, which subsequent editions of this book will be updated to include.

INDEX

INDEX

CREDITS

The publishers would like to thank the following sources for their kind permission to reproduce the pictures in this book. Key: T=top, B=bottom, L=left, R=right, C=centre.

COLORSPORT: 189; /Andrew Cowie: 188

THE FA: 21; /Lynne Cameron: 15B, 254, 255, 257TR, 267; /Getty Images: 11, 31B, 66BR, 209B, 215, 218T, 218BL, 218BR, 219, 220, 221, 222-223, 227B, 230; /Paul Greenwood: 257TL, 257BR; /Eddie Keogh/Getty Images: 7-6, 14B, 131, 227TR, 246, 247, 248T, 248B, 249, 250T, 250B, 251T, 251B, 253, 266; /Jed Leicester: 257BL, 258-259; /Matt Lewis/Getty Images: 224; /Kunjan Malde: 15T; /Eamonn McCormack/Getty Images: 242; /Simon Mooney/Mooneyphoto: 13B; /Mooneyphoto: 203T, 212, 213, 240

GETTY IMAGES: /AFP: 71B, 152B; /Allsport: 100, 150B, 159TL; /Odd Andersen/AFP: 204C; /Lars Baron/FIFA: 16-17, 238B; /Bentley Archive/Popperfoto: 103, 106; /Bettmann: 102TL, 104-105, 107T; /Reg Birkett/Keystone: 76; /Shaun Botterill: 203B, 205, 206, 208T; /Howard Boylan: 172B; /Clive Brunskill: 130, 191; /Simon Bruty: 160; /Gareth Cattermole/FIFA: 256; /Central Press: 77C, 81B, 89TL, 98B, 102TR, 109TL, 112T; /Graham Chadwick: 196T; /Chris Cole: 170B; /Phil Cole: 214B; /Frank Coppi/Popperfoto: 173; /Kevin C Cox/FIFA: 239T; /Ronald Dumont/Daily Express: 143; /Evening Standard: 93B, 94R; /Express: 67, 94TR, 127T; /Terry Fincher/Keystone: 78; /Stu Forster: 8, 175T, 178T, 194; /Monte Fresco/Mirrorpix: 89TR; /Monte Fresco/Topical Press Agency: 64; /Lluis Gene/AFP: 202; /George Greenwell/Mirrorpix: 87; /Laurence Griffiths: 252; /Martin Hayhow/AFP: 166; /Haynes Archive/Popperfoto: 53; /Hulton Archive: 12, 50, 75, 102B, 111B; /Hulton-Deutsch Collection/Corbis: 73B, 74B; /Imagno: 48T, 48B, 49; /Keystone: 71T, 101TL; /Ross Kinnaird: 179T, 200T, 200B, 208B; /Toshifumi Kitamura/AFP: 201; /Christof Koepsel: 234, 239B; /Ed Lacey/Popperfoto: 107B; /Eileen Langsley/Popperfoto: 185; /Mark Leech/Offside: 169B, 178B, 226; /Dominic Lipinski: 243; /Alex Livesey: 233; /John MacDougall/AFP: 214T; /Clive Mason: 204T, 217; /Antony Matheus Linsen/Fairfax Media: 141; /Eammon McCabe/Popperfoto: 124; /John McDonald: 225; /Douglas Miller/Keystone: 80; /Mirrorpix: 66BL, 109R, 112B, 151; /Don Morley: 65, 66T, 95, 118, 121T; /Gray Mortimore: 165T; /Steve Morton: 167T; /Bradley Ormesher/Mirrorpix: 209T; /PNA Rota: 79B; /Picture Post: 13T; /Joern Pollex: 216B; /Paul Popper/Popperfoto: 167B, 195; /Popperfoto: 22, 23T, 24, 25, 26, 29L, 30, 31T, 36, 42T, 47, 52T, 60, 61B, 62, 70, 79T, 81T, 84, 85, 88. 89B, 92, 98T, 99, 101BL, 101TR, 111T, 113T, 115T, 115C, 115B, 116T, 116BL, 117, 119, 121B, 136-137, 156T, 175B, 196B; /Gary M Prior: 190; /Professional Sport/Popperfoto: 14T, 159TR, 176-177; /Duncan Raban/Popperfoto: 164; /Ben Radford: 174, 197, 198BL, 198-199, 207T; /Rolls Press/Popperfoto: 101L, 101BR, 108T, 108B, 116BR; /Ian Showell/Keystone: 138, 139T; /Dan Smith: 165B; /Reg Speller: 94TL; /Cameron Spencer: 216T; /Patrik Stollarz/AFP: 238T; /Bob Thomas: 152T, 153, 170T, 204B, 207B, 227TL; /Bob Thomas/Popperfoto: 23B, 28, 29R, 35, 37, 38-39, 41T, 46, 122, 125, 126, 127T, 128, 129, 149, 150T, 154T, 154B, 156B, 157R, 158, 159B, 161T, 161B, 168, 169T, 179B, 183TR, 183B, 184; /Topical Press Agency: 51T; /ullstein bild: 52B, 59, 74T, 135T; /William Vanderson/Fox Photos: 73TL; /Walter Tull Archive/Finlayson Family Archive: 40; /Ian Walton: 235, 236-237, 241R

PA IMAGES: 58T, 86, 94B, 145, 171; /Matthew Ashton: 231, 232; /Ron Bella: 13C, 93T; /DPA: 77T, 77B, 110; /Empics Sport: 20; /Ross Kinnaird: 157L, 172T; /Steve Mitchell: 241L; /Peter Robinson: 186T, 186B; /S&G and Barratts: 43R, 57, 58B, 61T, 63L, 63R, 72, 73TR, 139B, 142, 144; /Topfoto: 41B, 58C, 90, 91, 135B

SHUTTERSTOCK: /AP: 51B, 113B; /Colorsport: 27, 42B, 43L; /Monte Fresco/Daily Mail: 140; /Pete Lomas/ANL: 183TL

SPORTING GREATS: /Daryl Fletcher: 182, 187

Every effort has been made to acknowledge correctly and contact the source and/or copyright holder of each picture. Any unintentional errors or omissions will be corrected in future editions of this book.